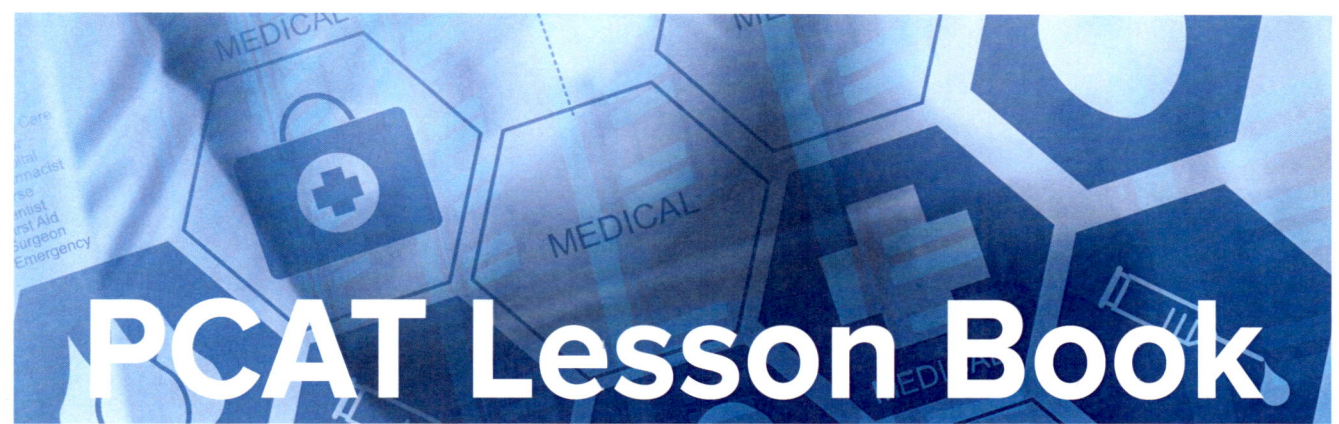

PCAT Lesson Book

Copyright 2018 by Next Step Test Preparation, LLC

All rights reserved. This book or any portion thereof may not be reproduced nor used in any manner whatsoever without the express written permission of the publisher, except for the use of brief quotations in a book review.

Printed in the United States of America

First Printing, 2018

ISBN 978-1-944935-27-6

Next Step Test Preparation, LLC
4256 N Ravenswood Ave
Suite 207
Chicago, IL 60613

www.nextsteptestprep.com

PCAT is a registered trademark of Pearson Education. Pearson has not reviewed nor endorsed this work in any way.

TABLE OF CONTENTS

Read This First! v

Lesson 1 1

Lesson 2 15

Lesson 3 27

Lesson 4 37

Lesson 5 49

Lesson 6 57

Lesson 7 67

Lesson 8 79

Lesson 9 89

Lesson 10 99

Lesson 11. 109

Lesson 12 121

Lesson 13 137

Lesson 14 147

Lesson 15 163

Lesson 16 179

Lesson 17 195

This page left intentionally blank.

STOP! READ THIS FIRST!

How to Use This Book

This book is a companion to the online videos for Next Step's PCAT course. It does not contain answers and explanations—or even an answer key. For this book to be of use, you must be a Next Step class student and be using it to follow along your Next Step PCAT classes.

The class sessions have been designed to be a mix of the three things needed for Test Day success: content review, question practice, and passage practice. While the class sessions do cover all of the high-yield strategies and content that you will need, this book is not complete prep by itself; you will only get value out of this book by watching the accompanying videos.

Every single class session has homework to be completed before the class, using your Next Step PCAT Review Book. To get the most out of the class lessons, you should keep up with the homework to be completed before and after each session.

Given the volume of homework to do, class lessons should be spaced out on a 1-to-3 times per week schedule. While it is possible to go through class lessons every other day (or even every day), working on such a compressed time scale will make it tough to do enough homework to get the most out of your prep.

Finally, you should take advantage of one of Next Step's unique class feature: live group office hours. Next Step conducts live office hours multiple times every month, giving you access to the most experienced PCAT teachers in the world—the ones that wrote your course! The live group office hours are conducted by teachers with the highest possible qualifications—years of experience, a 99th+ percentile score on the real PCAT, and experience writing and editing the Next Step course materials. If you find that you have a question that isn't answered by the books or videos, the group office hours let you get your questions answered.

Before diving into the lessons, be sure to complete the following preliminary steps:

1. Watch the orientation video the first time you log in at nextsteppcat.com
2. Complete the Next Step PCAT Diagnostic Test
3. Use the online Study Plan tool to set up your study calendar

This page left intentionally blank.

Introduction to PCAT Strategy

To Do Before Lesson 1

- ❑ Diagnostic Exam
- ❑ Read Chapter 1: Introduction

In Lesson 1

- > About the PCAT
- > Test Day
- > Building a Study Plan
- > Introduction to Content Review
- > Practice Preview

To Do After Lesson 1

- ❑ Review Diagnostic Exam
- ❑ Create a Study Plan
- ❑ Determine Target and Dream Scores
- ❑ Explore Next Step resources
- ❑ Explore Pearson PCAT website at *http://pcatweb.info/*
- ❑ Read Chapter 2: Writing

NextStep**TESTPREP**.com

About the PCAT

Exam Structure
- PCAT sections will always be in the same order: Writing, Biological Processes, Chemical Processes, Critical Reading, and Quantitative Reasoning
- Expect to take 3.5–4.0 hours to complete

Fill in the table with the number of questions and time allowed for each PCAT section.

SECTION	QUESTIONS	TIME
Writing		
Biological Processes		
Chemical Processes		
Rest Break		
Critical Reading		
Quantitative Reasoning		
Total	192 questions	240 min

Decide whether each of the following statements is true or false.

1. All sections are multiple-choice only.　　　　T　F
2. About 50% of the Quantitative questions will be word problems.　　　　T　F
3. The exam can be paused at any time.　　　　T　F
4. Organic chemistry is about 10% of the Chemical Processes Section.　　　　T　F
5. Trigonometry is tested in the Quantitative section.　　　　T　F

LESSON 1: INTRODUCTION TO PCAT STRATEGY

Exam Dates

> All PCAT exams are weighted on the same scale
> Register early (before late registration fee applies) at *http://pcatweb.info*
> Cancel registration before cancellation deadline for partial refund
> Administered at Pearson Testing Centers
> Arrive 30 minutes early
> You will receive a preliminary Score Report immediately after the exam
> You will receive an Official Score Report with your Writing score within 5 weeks after taking the exam

PCAT 2018–19 TESTING DATES	
Registration Window	**Testing Dates**
April 2—June 27	July 11, 18, 2018
April 2—July 6	September 6–7, 2018
September 5—October 5	October 22–31, 2018, November 1–2, 2018
April 2—November 2	January 3–4, 2019

Find the ideal Test Day for you.

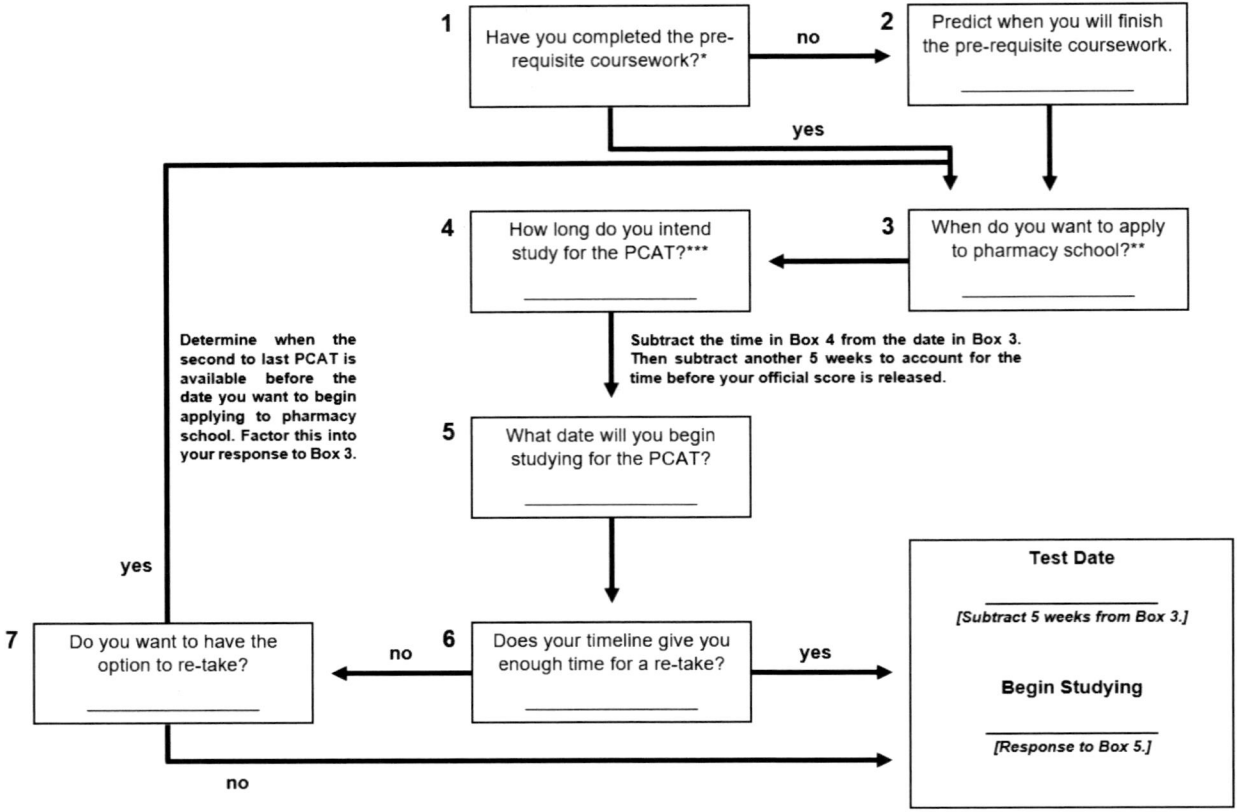

* 1-2 years of biology, 1 year of general chemistry, 1 year of organic chemistry, and 1 year of calculus

** Most pharmacy schools begin interviewing in September and October on a rolling admissions basis, so it is best to take the PCAT before then. Find the closest testing date before you apply.

*** Most students who are in school will study for at least 3–4 months, but students working full-time may study for 5–6 months or even longer.

Scoring

> You will receive a **scaled score (SS)** from 200–600 on each of the four multiple-choice sections and a 1–6 score on the Writing section. Your composite score will be the average of your four scaled scores. The mean PCAT score is a 400 with a standard deviation of 25.
> Your **percentile rank (PR)** indicates how you scored relative to all PCAT test-takers. Scaled scores and percentile rankings for each section of the PCAT are listed in Appendix A.
> Find a realistic Target Score by taking into account your Diagnostic score and the average scores of matriculants at the pharmacy schools you wish to attend.

Draw lines on the PCAT Score Distribution below to represent (A) your Diagnostic score, (B) your Target Score, and (C) your Dream Score.

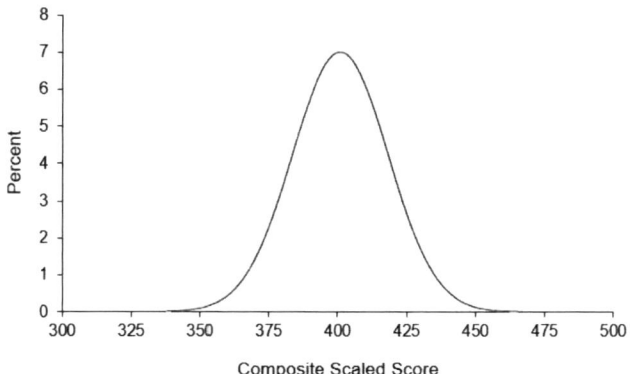

Fill out the sample Score Report below with your Target Scores.

MULTIPLE CHOICE	SCALED SCORE	PERCENTILE		SCORE	MEAN
Biological Processes			Writing		3.31
Chemical Processes					
Critical Reading					
Quantitative Reasoning					
Composite					

NextStepTESTPREP.com

Test Day

What to Bring

What items will you bring with you on Test Day?

- ❏ Two forms of identification: _____ and _____
- ❏ _____
- ❏ _____
- ❏ _____
- ❏ _____

What rules should you follow on Test Day?

- ❏ You should arrive _____ before your exam.
- ❏ You may only bring _____ into your testing room.
- ❏ Your cell phone and any electronic devices must be _____ during the exam and you __may / may not__ access them during the exam.
- ❏ During the rest break, you may only access _____ from your locker.

Test Day Tools

Check off each of the following tools once you feel comfortable using each.

- ❏ Dry-erase board and marker
- ❏ Standard online calculator
- ❏ Periodic table
- ❏ Countdown timer
- ❏ Flag for Review button
- ❏ Review Screen

Building a Study Plan

Study Schedule

1. Create a calendar in Excel, Google Sheets, or your personal calendar.

2. Mark Test Day and Day 1 of studying.

3. Reserve the day before Test Day and at least one day per week as rest days.

4. Mark out any days that you are unable or unwilling to study (travel, important exams, holidays, etc.).

5. Determine how many hours you are able to study each day of the week.

6. Determine how many Full-Length exams you will take and space them out equally between Day 1 and Test Day, with at least 4 days between each Full-Length. On average, most students will take one FL every other week.

7. The day after each Full-Length, reserve time to analyze your exam.

8. Predict how much time it will take you to complete each lesson and the pre-work for every lesson. Starting with Day 1, fill in your schedule with the days you intend to complete every lesson. Be conservative—leave extra time to catch up when you get behind, and give yourself time to do extra review and practice.

9. Fill in your schedule with the pre- and post-work for every lesson.

10. Write down "Review" on your calendar at least one day each week to remind yourself to regularly review this material.

11. After the last lesson is completed, divide the days remaining before Test Day into time for (1) content review, (2) practice questions, and (3) review of practice questions. You may need to be flexible because the areas you will need to review may change over the course of your study program.

12. In the week before Test Day, create a checklist for the goals you have that week (i.e., read X passages, review all flashcards, draw out important biochemical pathways, etc.).

13. In a side note, create a reminder for tasks you will complete regularly: content review, flashcards, Critical Reading passages, etc.

14. In another side note, create a reminder of all the resources you have access to so you don't forget about them!

NextStepTESTPREP.com

Sample Study Schedule

PCAT STUDY SCHEDULE

*Daily: 1-2 Critical Reading passages, 15 min. chemistry flashcards

		SUNDAY	MONDAY	TUESDAY	WEDNESDAY	THURSDAY	FRIDAY	SATURDAY
MAR	Week 10	26	DAY 1 **Diagnostic Exam**	review Diagnostic	Read Ch. 1 Complete Lesson 1	Lesson 1 post-work	Lesson 1 post-work REVIEW	REST DAY
	Week 9	5 Read Ch. 2 Complete Lesson 2	Writing Section Review	Read Ch. 28	Complete Lesson 3 Reading Section Review	Read Ch. 3-4	Read Ch. 5 REVIEW	REST DAY
	Week 8	12 **Full-Length 1**	review FL1	Complete Lesson 4 Start LLJ	Read Ch. 20	Read Ch. 21	Complete Lesson 5 REVIEW	REST DAY
	Week 7	19 Read Ch. 29 Develop Equation Sheet	Complete Lesson 6	*study for exam tomorrow*	Complete Lesson 7	Read Ch. 6-7	Read Ch. 8 REVIEW	REST DAY
	Week 6	26 **Full-Length 2**	review FL2	Complete Lesson 8	Read Ch. 22	Read Ch. 23	Complete Lesson 9 REVIEW	REST DAY
	Week 5	2 Read Ch. 30-31	Complete Lesson 10	Read Ch. 9	Read Ch. 10-11	Complete Lesson 11 Read Ch. 24	Read Ch. 25 REVIEW	REST DAY

Resources

Identify your go-to resources for each of the following.

Content Review

Practice Questions

LESSON 1: INTRODUCTION TO PCAT STRATEGY

Practice Passages

Online Resources

Flashcards

NextStepTESTPREP.com

Introduction to Content Review

> Every study program should have 3 elements:
> - _____
> - _____
> - _____

Match each activity with the type of content review it represents.

| Content Review |
| Practice |
| Review |

Practicing mathematics questions

Watching videos covering difficult content areas

Completing Critical Reading passages

Writing notes on a content review chapter

Taking a Full-Length exam

Reviewing flashcards

Completing End of Chapter Questions

Reading content review chapters

Analyzing the results of a Full-Length exam

Completing Section Reviews

Reviewing notes

Practice Preview

1. Which one of the following enzymes is involved in DNA replication in human cells?
   A. Taq polymerase
   B. RNA polymerase
   C. Ligase
   D. Transcriptase

2. Steroid hormones are composed of cholesterol. In order for the cell to produce these hormones, they must be processed correctly with the help of the smooth endoplasmic reticulum and secreted through the Golgi apparatus. Based on this, which of the organs would be expected to have cells with the largest smooth ER and Golgi apparatus?
   A. Anterior pituitary
   B. Pancreas
   C. Ovary
   D. Adrenal medulla

3. If a cell detects serious issues within replicated DNA, in which phase will it remain in to attempt to remedy it?
   A. G_1
   B. G_2
   C. S
   D. M

4. Which of the following molecules is most likely to be reabsorbed in the proximal convoluted tubule?
   A. Solute A, a small, vital biomolecule
   B. Solute B, a large protein that serves multiple essential functions
   C. Solute C, a medium-sized toxin
   D. Solute D, an ion with minor physiological uses

5. Of the below mechanisms, which best describes how gases, particularly oxygen and carbon dioxide, are exchanged between the alveoli and the blood?
   A. Simple diffusion
   B. Active transport
   C. Osmosis
   D. Facilitated diffusion

6. The one-letter code for lysine is:
   A. L
   B. K
   C. N
   D. Y

7. An unsaturated free fatty acid must contain:
   A. an alkene or alkyne.
   B. an ester.
   C. a carboxylic acid.
   D. two of the above.

8. The ratio of protons to neutrons in radon-222 is:
   A. 1:1
   B. 1:2
   C. 43:68
   D. 86:222

9. If a 0.2-kg sample contains 6.0×10^{26} molecules, what is its molar mass?
   A. 0.2 g/mol
   B. 0.5 g/mol
   C. 5 g/mol
   D. 20 g/mol

10. Write the balanced equation for the oxidation of zinc by hydrochloric acid.
    A. Zn_2 (s) + 4 HCl (aq) → 2 $ZnCl_4$ (aq) + 4 H^+ (aq)
    B. Zn (s) + 2 HCl (aq) → $ZnCl_2$ (aq) + 2 H^+ (aq)
    C. Zn (s) + 2 HCl (aq) → $ZnCl_2$ (aq) + H_2 (g)
    D. 2 Zn (s) + 2 HCl (aq) → Zn_2Cl_2 (aq) + H_2 (aq)

11. Solve $(12-9)4^2-1$.
    A. 27
    B. 45
    C. 47
    D. 143

12. Solve $\frac{1}{4} - \frac{7}{6} \times \frac{5}{6}$.
    A. $-\frac{13}{18}$
    B. $-\frac{67}{12}$
    C. $-\frac{55}{72}$
    D. $-\frac{55}{12}$

13. Solve $\log_3 27 = x$.
    A. x=3
    B. x=4
    C. x=6
    D. x=9

14. Factor the expression $3x^2+x-2$.
    A. $(3x+1)(x-2)$
    B. $(3x-1)(3x+2)$
    C. $(x-1)(3x+2)$
    D. $(x+1)(3x-2)$

15. Solve $(-3x/2) + 5 < (x/4) - 9$.
    A. x<8
    B. x>8
    C. x>−8
    D. x<−8

To Do After Lesson 1

- ❏ Review Diagnostic Exam
- ❏ Create a Study Plan
- ❏ Determine Target and Dream Scores
- ❏ Explore Next Step resources
- ❏ Explore Pearson PCAT website at *http://pcatweb.info/*
- ❏ Read Chapter 2: Writing

This page left intentionally blank.

Writing

LESSON 2

To Do Before Lesson 2

- ❏ Review Diagnostic Exam
- ❏ Create a Study Plan
- ❏ Determine Target and Dream Scores
- ❏ Explore Next Step resources
- ❏ Explore Pearson PCAT website at *http://pcatweb.info/*
- ❏ Read Chapter 2: Writing

In Lesson 2

- > Scoring
- > Language Conventions
- > Problem-Solving
- > Putting It All Together
- > Practice Cooldown

To Do After Lesson 2

- ❏ Complete Writing Section Review
- ❏ Read Chapter 28: Critical Reading

Scoring

> You will be given 30 minutes to respond to an essay prompt.
> Your essay will be scored on a scale from 1.0–6.0 from the average of two scores. The mean score of all test-takers is typically around 3.0–4.0.
> The prompt will present a contemporary _____ issue, _____ issue, or _____ issue and ask you to discuss a solution to this problem.

Fill in the table with the qualities of Superior (6), Effective (4), and Marginal (2) essays.

		6 SUPERIOR	4 EFFECTIVE	2 MARGINAL
Language Conventions	Errors			
	Structure			
Problem-Solving	Solutions			
	Support			
	Organization			

Language Conventions

Errors

Correct and identify the error type for the grammatical and spelling errors in the text.

> Errors: spelling, vocabulary, punctuation, capitalization, sentence formation, subject-verb agreement, pronoun agreement, faulty parallelism

Healthcare-associated infections cost taxpayers millions of dollars and causes thousands of preventable deaths in the United states each year. Not only are the economic and mortality concerns reason enough for alarm, these deaths are also largely preventable. Many of the patients whom will contract fetal infections are generally healthy or recovering from simple procedures but the combination of immunocompromised patients and a plethora of antibiotic-bugs makes healthcare settings breeding grounds for healthcare-associated infections. The number of annal Healthcare-associated infections can be eviscerated greatly by training healthcare professionals on basic hygiene protocols and prevent the over-prescription over antibiotics.

Solution:

Healthcare-associated infections cost taxpayers millions of
                              1
dollars and **cause** thousands of preventable deaths in the
              2
United **States** each year. Not only are the economic and
                                    3
mortality concerns reason enough for alarm, **but** these deaths
                                                4
are also largely preventable. Many of the patients **who** will
              5
contract **fatal** infections are generally healthy or recovering
                      6
from simple procedures, but the combination of

immunocompromised patients and a plethora of antibiotic
    7
-**resistant** bugs makes healthcare settings breeding grounds
                                              8
for healthcare-associated infections. The number of **annual**
       9   10
healthcare-associated infections can be **reduced** greatly by

training healthcare professionals on basic hygiene protocols
          11   12
and **preventing** the over-prescription **of** antibiotics.

---

1 subject-verb agreement
2 capitalization
3 sentence formation
4 pronoun agreement
5 vocabulary
6 punctuation
7 vocabulary
8 spelling
9 capitalization
10 vocabulary
11 faulty parallelism
12 vocabulary

Structure

Rewrite each of the sentences below to improve their structural pattern.

Training programs have been implemented by hospitals to reduce the number of preventable infections and improve patient outcomes.

_____

_____

_____

We know that basic hygiene protocols can directly contribute to a decline in the number of healthcare-associated infections because you are less likely to be in contact with bacteria and other infectious microbes, particularly at open wounds.

___

It is important that all members of the healthcare team receive up-to-date training on hand hygiene measures in order to prevent disease.

___

Not only should annual trainings be implemented nationwide, but I also think the success of these programs should be monitored and evaluated on a regular basis.

___

In this day and age, healthcare staff must have access to protocols that reduce the contamination risk at catheter sites and information about precautions to take with specific types of infectious diseases.

___

Problem-Solving

Solutions

Describe the problem discussed in the prompt below in your own words and elaborate on the issues posed by this problem.

Global sea levels have risen nearly 7 inches in the past century and continue to rise at a rate of 3.4 mm per year according to the National Aeronautics and Space Administration (NASA). Scientists predict that the sea level will rise another 1-4 feet by 2100. Discuss a solution to the problem of sea level rise caused by global warming.

Why is this a problem?

Pose as many solutions as you can to the problem discussed in the prompt above.

What solutions would address this problem?

1.

2.

3.

4.

5.

Support

Develop support and/or evidence for each of your solutions.

What support can you provide for each solution?

1.

2.

3.

4.

5.

Finally, synthesize and/or reconcile the solutions you proposed into a compelling conclusion or thesis.

What is your ultimate solution to the problem, and what outcome(s) do you expect?

Organization

Choose your best solutions and supporting information to briefly develop an outline for an essay response to the prompt.

```
I.     Introduction
         a. _____
         b. _____
         c. _____
II.    Body Paragraph 1
         a. _____
         b. _____
         c. _____
III.   Body Paragraph 2
         a. _____
         b. _____
         c. _____
IV.    Body Paragraph 3
         a. _____
         b. _____
         c. _____
V.     Conclusion
         a. _____
         b. _____
         c. _____
```

Putting It All Together

Plan your approach to the PCAT Writing Essay by filling in the strategic table below.

STEP	APPROACH	TIME
Reflect		
Outline		
Write		
Proofread		
Total		30 min

NextStepTESTPREP.com

Write the essay in the Writing Section Review in 30 minutes and answer the following.

	Yes	No
> Did I feel rushed or run out of time?	❏	❏
> Did I make any errors (spelling, grammar, sentence structure)?	❏	❏
> Did these mistakes interfere with the meaning or flow of the essay?	❏	❏
> Do I use the active or passive voice?	❏	❏
> Is the narrative voice consistent?	❏	❏
> Are there a variety of sentence structures?	❏	❏
> Is the writing concise?	❏	❏
> Is the problem discussed in detail?	❏	❏
> Do I provide multiple solutions and support them in detail?	❏	❏
> Does the essay transition seamlessly and have a logical organization?	❏	❏
> Does the introductory paragraph "hook" the reader?	❏	❏
> Have I synthesized the information in a powerful conclusion?	❏	❏
> Is my main argument effective?	❏	❏

Practice Cooldown

Analyze and score the following essay written in response to the prompt below.

According to U.S. Centers for Disease Control, healthcare-associated infections cause more than 720,000 acute care visits each year, resulting in about 75,000 preventable patient deaths. Discuss a solution to the problem of preventing and reducing infections contracted in healthcare facilities.

Healthcare-associated infections cost taxpayers millions of dollars and cause thousands of preventable deaths in the United States each year. Not only are the economic and mortality concerns reason enough for alarm, but these deaths are also largely preventable. Many of the patients who will contract fatal infections are generally healthy or recovering from simple procedures, but the combination of immunocompromised patients and a plethora of antibiotic-bugs makes healthcare settings breeding grounds for healthcare-associated infections. The number of annual healthcare-associated infections can be reduced greatly by training healthcare professionals on basic hygiene protocols and preventing the over-prescription over antibiotics.

Basic hygiene protocols can directly contribute to a decline in the number of healthcare-associated infections by reducing the risk of bacteria and other infectious microbes coming into contact with patients, particularly at open wounds. Hospitals that have implemented annual training programs for their healthcare staff have seen drastic reductions in preventable infections and overall improvements in patient outcomes. It is important that all members of the healthcare team receive up-to-date training on hand hygiene measures, protocols that reduce the contamination risk at catheter sites, and information about precautions to take with specific types of infectious diseases. Not only should annual trainings be implemented nationwide, but the success of these programs should be monitored and evaluated on a regular basis to determine effective measures for reducing healthcare-associated infections.

Antibiotic control is another important consideration. Hospitals and clinics must strive to reduce the over-prescription of antibiotics. Some clinics have been successful tracking over-prescribers within their system and targeting them for education and training. Pediatric practices should be incentivized to develop seasonal educational programs that coincide with the flu season to equip their providers with the information needed to prescribe antibiotics wisely. By doing so, the risk of bacteria developing antibiotic resistance is greatly reduced, thus also helping preventing countless healthcare-associated infections each year.

While basic hygiene protocols and antibiotic regulation each on their own will help, together these two preventative measures have great potential to significantly impact patients, healthcare systems, and taxpayers for the better. The former requires cooperation within a healthcare team, and the latter requires cooperation between a physician and patient. One day, healthcare-associated infections may be a thing of the past.

	STRENGTHS	WEAKNESSES
Errors		
Structure		
Solution		
Support		
Organization		

OVERALL SCORE

To Do After Lesson 2

- ❏ Complete Writing Section Review
- ❏ Read Chapter 28: Critical Reading

Critical Reading 1

To Do Before Lesson 3
- ❏ Complete Writing Section Review
- ❏ Read Chapter 28: Critical Reading

In Lesson 3
> Passage Strategy
> Passage Practice
> Practice Cooldown

To Do After Lesson 3
- ❏ Critical Reading Section Review
- ❏ Read Biological Processes Ch. 3–5
- ❏ Complete BP Ch. 3–5 End of Chapter Questions

Passage Strategy

Timing

- You will have _____ minutes to answer _____ questions (_____ passages each associated with _____ questions). This gives you approximately _____ minutes to complete each passage and its questions.
- Try several approaches:
  - <u>Speed Read</u>: 2 min reading + 4 min answering questions
  - <u>Even-Split</u>: 3 min reading + 3 min answering questions
  - <u>Passage Mastery</u>: 4 min reading + 2 min answering questions
- Clock management
  - Be _____, not reactive
  - Check time every ~2–3 passages
  - Allow time to return to marked questions at the end

Active Reading

- Focus on _____, not complicated strategies.
- Reading passages should be an _____ process. Make mental notes of:
  - Key words
  - Opinions
  - Contrast
  - Main ideas or arguments
- **Avoid** note-taking as this is time-consuming. The PCAT rewards your understanding of main ideas, and you can always go back for details.
- **Avoid** skipping passages as this is also time-consuming, and it is difficult to evaluate the difficulty of a passage with a brief glace.
- Reflect periodically to ensure that you understand the author's thesis and the arguments supporting that position.

Highlight key words, opinions, contrast, and main ideas in the text below.

The needs that are usually taken as the starting point for motivation theory are the so-called physiological drives. Two recent lines of research make it necessary to revise our customary notions about these needs: first, the development of the concept of homeostasis, and second, the finding that appetites (preferential choices among foods) are a fairly efficient indication of actual needs or lacks in the body.

Thus, it seems impossible as well as useless to make any list of fundamental physiological needs for they can come to almost any number one might wish, depending on the degree of specificity of description. We cannot identify all physiological needs as homeostatic. That sexual desire, sleepiness, sheer activity and maternal behavior in animals, are homeostatic, has not yet been demonstrated. Furthermore, this list would not include the various sensory pleasures (tastes, smells, tickling, stroking) which are probably physiological and which may become the goals of motivated behavior.

In a previous paper, it has been pointed out that these physiological drives or needs are to be considered unusual rather than typical because they are isolable, and because they are localizable somatically. That is to say, they are relatively independent of each other, of other motivations and of the organism as a whole, and secondly, in many cases, it is possible to demonstrate a localized, underlying somatic base for the drive. This is true less generally than has been thought (exceptions are fatigue, sleepiness, maternal responses), but it is still true in the classic instances of hunger, sex, and thirst.

It should be pointed out again that any of the physiological needs and the consummatory behavior involved with them serve as channels for all sorts of other needs as well. That is to say, the person who thinks he is hungry may actually be seeking more for comfort, or dependence, than for vitamins or proteins. Conversely, it is possible to satisfy the hunger need in part by other activities such as drinking water or smoking cigarettes. In other words, relatively isolable as these physiological needs are, they are not completely so.

Undoubtedly these physiological needs are the most pre-potent of all needs. What this means specifically is, that in the human being who is missing everything in life in an extreme fashion, it is most likely that the major motivation would be the physiological needs rather than any others. A person who is lacking food, safety, love, and esteem would most probably hunger for food more strongly than for anything else.

[Adapted from "A Theory of Human Motivation", *Psychological Review*, by A.H. Maslow, 1943.]

Main Ideas

1.

2.

3.

4.

5.

Thesis:

Panic Mode

> With only a few minutes remaining, skim passages by reading the first and last sentence of each paragraph before quickly answering the questions.

Practice the Panic Mode approach by reading the passage below in 2 minutes.

In his recent book, *The Genius of Dogs: How Dogs are Smarter than You Think*, Brian Hare argues that the communicative abilities of dogs extend well past the blunt signifiers of tail and ear position and bared teeth that humans have long known. If you ask the typical lay person, they would suggest that dog vocalizations consist of little more than barking, growling, and whining. And while Hare's work doesn't expand on this basic repertoire, he convincingly argues that dogs are communicating far more than we were previously aware, through some combination of pitch, loudness and timbre.

Even many dog owners think that a dog's bark contains very little information. That is, the dog isn't "thinking" anything in particular, nor trying to communicate anything in particular. They bark just because "that's what dogs do". Research by Raymond Coppinger seems to support what he calls an "arousal model". That is, dogs simply bark when they're excited about something, and the barking is not a behavior over which the dog is exerting any conscious control and with no attempt at communication by the dog. In support of his hypothesis, Coppinger presents data gathered from several different breeds of working dogs whose job is to protect free-range livestock. In many instances, the dogs barked nearly continuously for six to eight hours, even when no other dogs or humans were within earshot. The bark simply communicates the fact that the barking dog is excited, with no attempt to communicate that message to any particular audience. Hare provides an anecdote which seems to align with the arousal model: he talks about a guard dog he had while working in Africa who would bark at every passerby throughout the night, even when they were people the dog had known and lived with for years.

More recent research, however, suggests that barking and growling may communicate more than had been previously thought. Dogs' vocal cords are highly flexible, permitting dogs to alter their vocalizations to produce a wide variety of different sounds. Scientists recorded the barking and growling done by dogs under a variety of situations. One involved a recording of a "food growl" and a "stranger growl". The first was recorded when researchers attempted to take food away from an aggressive dog, and the second when they simply approached aggressive dogs. They then placed food on the opposite side of the room from another dog and let it approach the food. They played back recordings of both the "stranger" and "food" growls as the dogs approached the food. Only in response to the "food" growl did the dogs hesitate before continuing.

In a similar experiment, researchers recorded the barks of dogs in two different situations. In the first, the dogs were simply left alone. In the second, a stranger would approach the dog, eliciting barking. When those barks were played later for other dogs, these other dogs ignored all of the "alone" barking, but perked up immediately when the "stranger" bark was played. Even more surprising, humans were able to distinguish between the barks, and correctly identify which was which, even if the human test subjects were not themselves dog owners.

Hare also notes that barking behavior itself seems to be an unintended consequence of domestication. While wolves and dogs share many behavioral characteristics (and, in fact, dogs were reclassified in 1993 as a subspecies of wolf), wolves rarely bark. Barking makes up only a small percent—by Hare's estimates as low as 3%—of wolf vocalizations. In addition, the experimental foxes in Russia that have been "force domesticated" over the span of just a handful of generations have shown the same split: the wild-type foxes don't bark, whereas the domesticated ones do. The artificial selection process that selects against aggression and fear in canids seems to have unearthed a propensity for barking.

[Adapted from "Sparky Speaks?" by Elliot Hirsen, 2011]

Main Ideas

1.

2.

3.

4.

5.

Thesis:

Passage Practice

Timed vs. Untimed

The key to mastering the Critical Reading section is _____!

Use **timed** practice to: _____

Use **untimed** practice to: _____

When can you commit to practicing Critical Reading passages? Daily? Once a week?

What are 3 goals or skills you would like to improve on in the Critical Reading section?

Review and Analysis

> Investigate **broad patterns or trends** and develop **actionable goals**.
> Keep track of trends in your performance over time in your Lessons Learned Journal.

Complete the Critical Reading Section Review and answer the following questions. In the future, record these responses in your Lessons Learned Journal.

> *Did I feel rushed or run out of time? If so, how can I improve my efficiency?*
> *Did I make any mistakes? Why did I make those mistakes?*
> *What strategies did I apply? Did they work?*

- *What strategies would I like to try?*
- *Did I return to the passage while answering questions? Did that help?*
- *Did I skip any passages or questions? Did I leave any questions unanswered?*
- *Were some passages harder than others? Did I answer a disproportionate number of questions incorrectly on certain passages?*
- *Were there any types of questions that I answered incorrectly more than other types of questions?*
- *For each question I missed, why did I select the incorrect answer?*
- *For each question I missed, can I point to evidence in the passage text that leads to the correct answer?*

Practice Cooldown

Read the following passage and answer the practice questions below.

European investigators have endeavored to discover the influence of climate, season, weather, age, sex, marriage, profession, religion, upon suicide. These statistical tables are valuable. We require, however: (1) A separate table for those undoubtedly insane, putting in a class by themselves those sane enough to lie influenced by rational motives. (2) Under religion, those who really believe in some creed should be distinguished from those nominally attached to it. (3) There should be a table of statistics of the divorced. (4) There should be an earnest attempt made to get beneath the statistics to the hidden influences—the 'moral causes.'

The commission and report by the Prussian government on suicides among school children indicates the need of similar inquiries into the causes and conditions leading to adult suicides. This might lead to insights that would guide preventive measures. These investigations should take into account the following: Physiological. The influence of epileptic, neurotic, dissipated parents. Influence of nerve exhausting vices, of mental overwork, of monotonous employment, of sedentary occupations. Psychical: The influence of monotony, of excitement, of excessive pursuit of wealth or pleasure, of disappointments, worries, of gambling. Literature: The influence of morbid sentimentalism in poetry and prose representing death as extinction, ignoring or denying the moral element in life conduct and destiny. The influence of dramatic representations of suicide, sometimes as in the case of Romeo and Juliet as the tragic ending of passionate love. The influence of realistic accounts of suicide in the newspapers, sometimes, it is claimed, initiating imitative epidemics. Social. The influence of solitariness, loneliness, brooding. The presence or absence of social or family ties. The sex instinct and the effect of the perversion or thwarting of this.

Then it might be in order to try to find out to what extent and in what ways educational, social, moral, or religious influences cooperate with the hygienic in keeping men and women in physical and mental health and normal, sane, and suitable activity. Even from the present data we may get some fairly obvious suggestions. Many suicides are undoubtedly insane, others are in the incipient stages, obsessed with various 'phobias' and probably all are in some degree morbid. Might not much be accomplished if we could succeed in convincing people of the hopefulness of cure and the need of expert advice and assistance in checking the earlier stages of threatened insanity? At present there is widespread despair.

Suicide accompanies civilization and education as an unerring index of maladjustment in society and defects in education. True education acts as a deterrent in teaching self-control, and in giving objective interests, literary, artistic, scientific, philosophical, philanthropic, moral, religious. The perverting influence of the realistic newspaper accounts of suicide should be checked by legislation.

[Adapted from "The Significance of Suicide", *Philosophical Review*, by James Gibson Hume, 1910.]

LESSON 3: CRITICAL READING 1

Main Ideas

1.

2.

3.

4.

Thesis:

1. What was the author's goal in writing this passage?
   A. To make the argument that government needs to put a stop to newspaper accounts of suicide.
   B. To discredit existing studies of suicide which fail to take into account many major factors.
   C. To clearly delineate the division between the truly insane and rational depressives.
   D. To suggest and detail prospective future studies of the factors influencing suicide.

2. Which of the following factors in suicide did the author NOT discuss in detail?
   A. Divorce
   B. Physiological conditions
   C. Representations of suicide in art and media
   D. Social ties

3. Which of the following, if true, would weaken the author's argument of suicide acting as a social "index", as discussed in the last paragraph?
   A. A large-scale study in Norway finds a correlation between hours of daylight and suicide rates.
   B. A longitudinal study of one US city reveals increases in suicide rates coincide with the onset of economic recessions.
   C. A French study reveals that survivors of failed suicide attempts are two percent less likely to make an additional attempt for each week of treatment received.
   D. A Canadian study reveals that the nation's highest rates of suicide all occur in populations over 1000 people with the lowest levels of crime and unemployment.

4. In order to decrease suicide rates, the author would probably agree that governments should:
   A. focus on treatment of those who have previously attempted suicide.
   B. devote funds to community wellness initiatives.
   C. sponsor a crisis response unit.
   D. increase prescription rates amongst community doctors.

To Do After Lesson 3

- ❑ Critical Reading Section Review
- ❑ Read Biological Processes Ch. 3–5
- ❑ Complete BP Ch. 3–5 End of Chapter Questions

Lesson 4: Biological Processes 1

To Do Before Lesson 4
- ❏ Critical Reading Section Review
- ❏ Read Biological Processes Ch. 3–5
- ❏ Complete BP Ch. 3–5 End of Chapter Questions

In Lesson 4
- > Study Groups
- > Lessons Learned Journal
- > Note-Taking and Study Sheets
- > Mnemonics
- > Spaced Repetition

To Do After Lesson 4
- ❏ Develop an LLJ
- ❏ Read Chemical Processes Ch. 20–21
- ❏ Complete CP Ch. 20–21 End of Chapter Questions

NextStepTESTPREP.com

Study Groups

- Start early!
- Group of 2–3, class members
- Meet regularly (at least once a week) in person or by web conference
- Have a plan
  - Identify group representative to email date, time, and location reminders
  - Choose a study group leader for each meeting
  - Review content and/or passages
  - Identify "lessons learned" from each passage together
  - Assign homework

How would a study group benefit you? What are the pros and cons?

Can you think of anyone you would like to have in your study group?

Lessons Learned Journal

> Develop an LLJ in a Word document, Excel spreadsheet, bound journal, etc.
> What is a "Lesson Learned"?
  - High-yield concepts
  - Helpful mnemonics
  - Strategy notes
  - Anything you want to do (or *not* do) on Test Day
> How to use the LLJ
  - Record Lessons Learned after completing any passage or content review
  - Review entire LLJ at the end of each week
  - Can be 25–100 pages long by the time you are done!

Draw the stages of mitosis and meiosis for a diploid (2N) cell with 4 chromosomes.

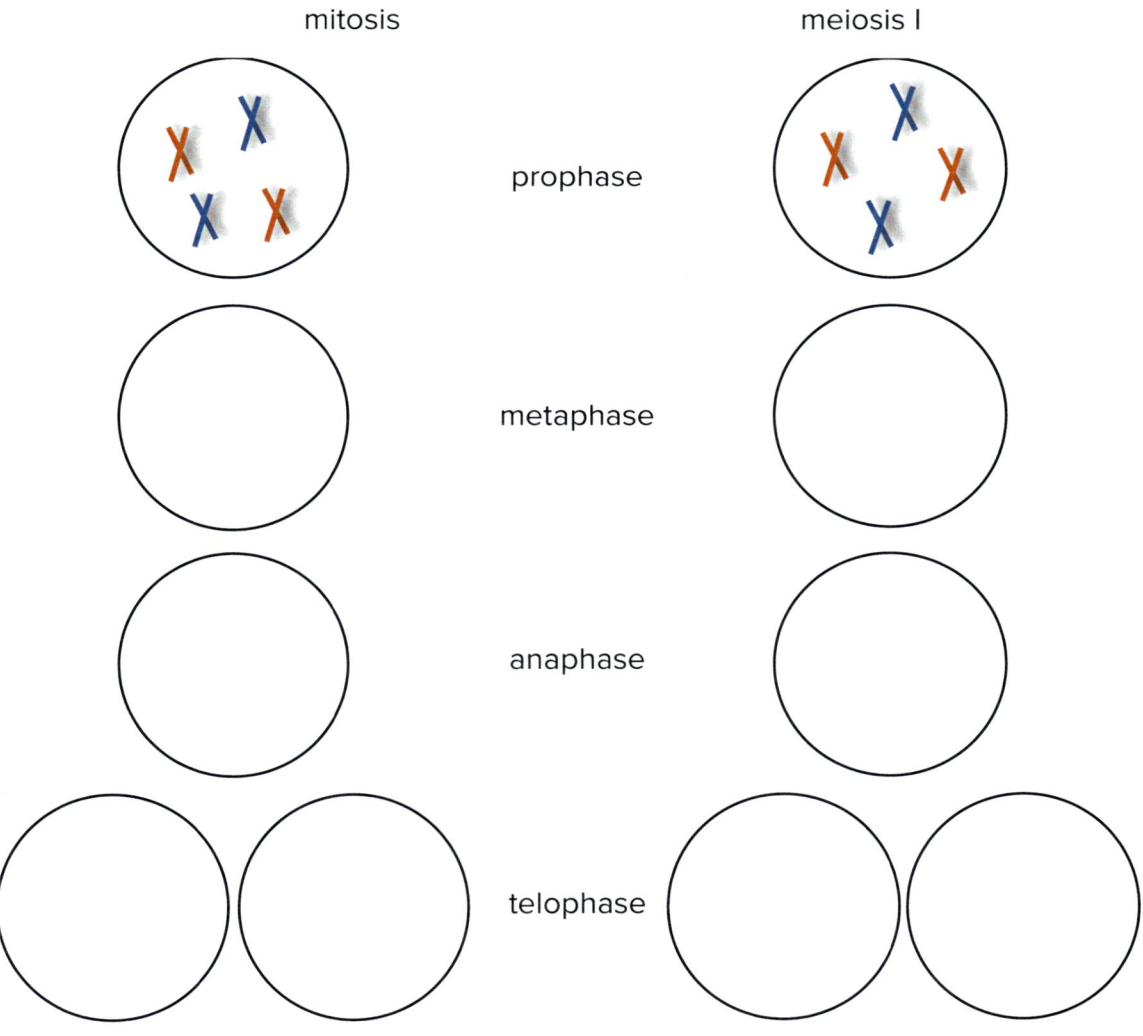

meiosis II

prophase

metaphase

anaphase

telophase

Record any Lessons Learned that will help you remember the differences and similarities between mitosis and meiosis.

Note-Taking

- ❏ Avoid passive methods!
- ❏ Take notes in the form of questions
- ❏ Create your own examples
- ❏ Draw diagrams and use visual tools
- ❏ Develop study sheets
  - Condense material onto one page
  - Make it easy to read and use color-coding
  - Collaborate and share with your study group

Write questions whose answers are the names of organelles.

Question: _____

Answer: Nucleus

Question: _____

Answer: Mitochondria

Question: _____

Answer: Lysosome

Question: _____

Answer: Golgi apparatus

Question: _____

Answer: Rough endoplasmic reticulum

Question: _____

Answer: Smooth endoplasmic reticulum

Write down or draw an example of each type of cellular transport.

Facilitated Diffusion

Primary Active Transport

Secondary Active Transport

Draw a diagram of each type of vesicle-mediated transport.

Endocytosis

Pinocytosis

Exocytosis

Mnemonics

❑ Good ones are outrageous, humorous, or related to people you know (or all 3!)
❑ Can be visual, auditory, kinesthetic

List any mnemonics you can think of that would be helpful for Biological Processes.

```
[                                                                              ]
```

Create mnemonics to help you remember each of the following.

Spermatozoa Pathway

Seminiferous tubules → Epididymis → Vas deferens → Ejaculatory ducts → Urethra → Penis

```
[                                                                              ]
```

Embryonic Cleavage

Zygote → Morula → Blastula → Gastrula

```
[                                                                              ]
```

Germ Layers

Ectoderm, Mesoderm, and Endoderm

```
[                                                                              ]
```

Spaced Repetition

- ❏ To consolidate memory, you must do two things: _____ and _____

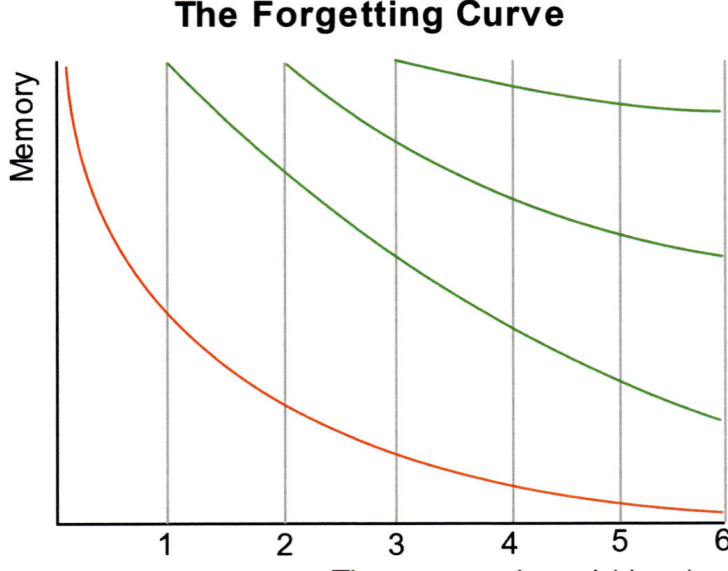

Image from: https://en.wikipedia.org/wiki/Forgetting_curve#/media/File:ForgettingCurve.svg (Public Domain)

- ❏ Review End of Chapter Questions:
    - At the end of the day
    - The next day
    - The next week

When can you commit to reviewing End of Chapter Questions? On Fridays? First thing in the morning?

Draw and label the stages of mitosis and meiosis for a diploid (2N) cell with 4 chromosomes . . . from memory!

Practice Cooldown

1. "Cell drinking" is also known as:
   A. endocytosis.
   B. minicytosis.
   C. phagocytosis.
   D. pinocytosis.

2. Which of the following statements regarding interphase is incorrect?
   A. DNA replication occurs during this time.
   B. The cell increases in size by way of continued protein synthesis.
   C. It encompasses more time in the cell cycle than other phases.
   D. The duration of each of its component phases is equal.

3. Unrestricted cell division is a hallmark of cancer cells. What is a reasonable explanation for this characteristic?
   A. Cancer cells can facilitate angiogenesis.
   B. Cancer cells rely on anaerobic respiration for ATP.
   C. Cancer cells can metastasize.
   D. Cancer cells lack cell cycle checkpoints.

4. What consequence is most likely if the Golgi apparatus were removed from a cell?
   A. The cell would no longer be able to target transmembrane proteins to the cell membrane as opposed to the nuclear membrane.
   B. The cell would no longer be able to properly excrete proteins.
   C. The cell would be incapable of forming lysosomes.
   D. All of the above would occur.

5. A student researcher accidentally injects the contents of a lysosome into his frog embryos. What will happen to one of these embryonic cells?
   A. The injected contents will be absorbed into the current lysosomes in the cell.
   B. The injected contents will be expelled by the frog embryo.
   C. The injected contents will begin to digest other proteins and macromolecules in the cell, possibly resulting in its death.
   D. The injected contents will be digested by the embryo.

6. What is the cellular function of smooth ER?
   A. To produce intracellular proteins
   B. To produce enzymes used in the degradation of cellular materials
   C. To synthesize or function in the synthesis of lipids and fatty acids
   C. To package proteins and lipids into vesicles

7. What is the most likely evolutionary advantage of the uneven cytoplasmic division that is seen during oogenesis?
   A. Only one egg is produced at a time, avoiding multiple births in animals that are not equipped to have a large number of offspring at one time.
   B. It slows the rate of reproduction, preventing overpopulation.
   C. It lessens the chance that genetic mutations will be passed on to the offspring.
   D. Oogenesis does not involve uneven division of the cytoplasm.

8. A human cell has only 13 chromosomes. What type of cell is it?
   A. A muscle cell
   B. A germ cell
   C. A diploid cell
   D. A somatic cell

9. The single diploid cell formed when an ovum is fertilized by a spermatozoon is known as a(n):
   A. embryo.
   B. zygote.
   C. morula.
   D. gastrula.

10. The heart is derived from which germ layer?
    A. Endoderm
    B. Ectoderm
    C. Cardioderm
    D. Mesoderm

To Do After Lesson 4

- ❏ Develop an LLJ
- ❏ Read Chemical Processes Ch. 20–21
- ❏ Complete CP Ch. 20–21 End of Chapter Questions

This page left intentionally blank.

Chemical Processes 1

LESSON 5

To Do Before Lesson 5
- ❏ Develop an LLJ
- ❏ Read Chemical Processes Ch. 20–21
- ❏ Complete CP Ch. 20–21 End of Chapter Questions

In Lesson 5
> The Tough Stuff
> Lessons Learned Journal
> Note-Taking and Study Sheets
> Mnemonics
> Spaced Repetition
> Practice Cooldown

To Do After Lesson 5
- ❏ Develop an Equation Sheet
- ❏ Read Quantitative Reasoning Ch. 29
- ❏ Complete QR Ch. 29 End of Chapter Questions

The Tough Stuff

> Identify learning strategies that are effective for you
> - Trifecta of *reading*, *writing*, and *videos*
> - Auditory, kinetic, and visual strategies
> - Flashcards and study sheets
> - Teach-back
> - Active learning and practice
>
> Make sure you understand the tough stuff before moving on
>
> Assess your understanding with practice questions
>
> Review material regularly
>
> Get help at a Next Step Office Hours session!

What are the three hardest PCAT topics you have studied so far?

Identify one of those topics. Re-read the chapter notes on this topic. Then, without looking back at the chapter, write succinct notes here from memory.

How did you do? Complete your notes with any other vital information that is missing. Do you have any questions about this topic that you don't have answers to? Hopefully you found that you captured the big picture and recalled the most high-yield information.

Outside resources can be an important part of learning complex topics. If you can you find an online video that explains this topic, write down the title of the video, where you found it, and how effective the video was in augmenting your understanding.

If possible, draw a sketch of this difficult topic. Use arrows, labels, and color coding to reinforce your learning.

Find and complete 5 practice problems that test you on this difficult topic, such as the End of Chapter Questions. What percentage did you answer correctly? Did you learn anything new from reviewing these questions?

Write down and answer three practice questions that could be asked on the PCAT about this topic.

1.

2.

3.

LESSON 5: CHEMICAL PROCESSES 1

Without your notes, teach this topic to a friend or record yourself teaching a lesson on this topic to your computer. How long did this take? What are the pros and cons to this technique?

```
┌─────────────────────────────────────────────────────────────────────┐
│                                                                     │
│                                                                     │
│                                                                     │
│                                                                     │
└─────────────────────────────────────────────────────────────────────┘
```

After completing these exercises, rank the review strategies from most to least helpful.

1. _____   Reading

2. _____   Writing

3. _____   Video

4. _____   Drawing

5. _____   Practice

6. _____   Teach-Back

Problem-Solving

> Look for shortcuts ... but be careful
>   – Elimination
>   – Estimation
>   – Work backwards
> Make logical connections
> There are only so many ways a question can be asked
> Learn, see, do: practice makes perfect!
> Check your work

Use the long method to determine the electron configuration of the following elements.

Ar   _____

Br   _____

Pd   _____

Ba   _____

K   _____

Cl⁻   _____

Use the shortcut (periodic table blocks) to determine the electron configuration of the following elements.

Ar   _____

Br   _____

Pd   _____

Ba   _____

K   _____

Cl⁻   _____

Practice Cooldown

1. A sample of earth from a recently discovered cave is found to contain a significant amount of ^{238}U. How many protons does one atom of this element have?
   A. 92
   B. 119
   C. 146
   D. 238

2. All of the following are true regarding the relationship between carbon and boron EXCEPT:
   A. carbon has a lesser electron affinity than boron.
   B. carbon has a greater ionization energy than boron.
   C. carbon is more electronegative than boron.
   D. carbon has a smaller atomic radius than boron.

3. Why are noble gases unreactive in nature?
   A. They form stable diatomic molecules.
   B. They possess complete valence shells.
   C. The have highly stable half-full valence shells.
   D. They tend to exist in an inert crystalline form.

4. A set of four quantum numbers can describe all of the following EXCEPT:
   A. the electron shell and subshell of an atom.
   B. the specific orbital of a subshell.
   C. the angular momentum of an electron.
   D. the charge density of an atom.

5. Which of the following bonds would exhibit the most ionic character?
   A. A single bond between F and O
   B. A single bond between B and S
   C. A single bond between H and N
   D. A single bond between Li and Cl

6. How many molecules of product form when 5 molecules of barium nitrate completely react with an excess of sulfuric acid?

$$Ba(NO_3)_2 \text{ (aq)} + H_2SO_4 \text{ (aq)} \rightarrow BaSO_4 \text{ (s)} + HNO_3 \text{ (aq)}$$

   A. 5 molecules
   B. 10 molecules
   C. 15 molecules
   D. Not enough information is given.

7. In an experiment, 50 mg of methane and 60 mg of sulfate are mixed in a closed container. What is the limiting reagent?

$$CH_4 (g) + SO_4^{2-} (aq) \rightarrow H_2O(l) + HS^- (aq) + HCO_3^- (aq)$$

   A. CH_4
   B. SO_4^{2-}
   C. HS^-
   D. HCO_3^-

8. Write the balanced equation for the oxidation of zinc by hydrochloric acid.
   A. $Zn_2 (s) + 4 HCl (aq) \rightarrow 2 ZnCl_4 (aq) + 4 H^+ (aq)$
   B. $Zn (s) + 2 HCl (aq) \rightarrow ZnCl_2 (aq) + 2 H^+ (aq)$
   C. $Zn (s) + 2 HCl (aq) \rightarrow ZnCl_2 (aq) + H_2 (g)$
   D. $2 Zn (s) + 2 HCl (aq) \rightarrow Zn_2Cl_2 (aq) + H_2 (aq)$

9. What is the electron configuration for Sr^{2+}?
   A. [Kr]
   B. [Kr] $4s^2$
   C. [Kr] $5s^2$
   D. [Kr] $5s^2 4d^2$

10. The structure of epinephrine contains how many sp^3-hybridized carbons?

   A. 3
   B. 4
   C. 6
   D. 9

To Do After Lesson 5

- ❏ Develop an Equation Sheet
- ❏ Read Quantitative Reasoning Ch. 29
- ❏ Complete QR Ch. 29 End of Chapter Questions

Lesson 6: Quantitative Reasoning 1

To Do Before Lesson 6
- ❏ Develop Equation Sheet
- ❏ Read Quantitative Reasoning Ch. 29
- ❏ Complete QR Ch. 29 End of Chapter Questions

In Lesson 6
- > Identifying Strengths
- > Lessons Learned Journal
- > Note-Taking and Study Sheets
- > Mnemonics
- > Practice
- > Practice Cooldown

To Do After Lesson 6
- ❏ Complete Full-Length 1
- ❏ Review Full-Length 1

Identifying Strengths

> Use End of Chapter Questions to identify your strengths
> Something can *always* be improved
   - Accuracy
   - Efficiency
   - Timing
> Use study groups to help identify strengths and tackle areas for improvement

What are your strengths in the Quantitative Reasoning section?

What skills would you like to improve?

Find the most accurate *and the most* efficient *methods to solve the following problems.*

	accurate method	efficient method

What is 145×33?

What is $\sqrt{50}$?

What is $\frac{14}{3} \times 0.26$?

LESSON 6: QUANTITATIVE REASONING 1

Lessons Learned Journal

> Specialize your LLJ for the Quantitative Reasoning section
  - New Excel sheet
  - Color coding by content type or by difficulty
> What is a "Lesson Learned" in the Quantitative Reasoning section?
  - High-efficiency shortcuts
  - Must-know equations
  - Helpful mnemonics
  - Strategy notes
  - Anything you want to do (or *not* do) on Test Day
> How to use the LLJ
  - Focus on high-yield strategies
  - Review entire LLJ at the end of each week
  - Do any strategies apply to multiple content areas?

Write the following values in scientific notation.

167001000   _____

0.00023   _____

12.45   _____

Record a Lesson Learned that will help you remember the rules for scientific notation.

Use unit conversion to convert from 96 inches to kilometers (1 in = 2.54 cm).

Record a Lesson Learned that will help you remember the rules for unit conversion.

Note-Taking

> - Some content will be "easy" but some will be harder
> - Show model examples in your notes
>   - Divide page into a column for notes and a column for equations
> - Learning equations
>   - Study sheets
>   - Flashcards
>   - Use color-coding
>   - Practice, practice, practice!

Fill in the sample notes on converting between decimals, fractions, and percents.

Notes	Examples
1. decimals → percents	_____
2. _____	23% ÷ 100% = 0.23
3. decimals → fractions	_____
4. fractions → decimals	_____
5. _____	$\frac{4}{5} = 0.8 \times 100\% = 80\%$
6. percents → fractions	_____

Fill in the table below with the properties of logarithms.

PROPERTY	EQUATION	EXAMPLE
Product Rule	$\log_b(xy) = \log_b(x) + \log_b(y)$	
Quotient Rule		$\log_{10}\left(\frac{1}{3}\right) = \log_{10} 1 - \log_{10}(3)$
Power Rule		

Mnemonics

> Good ones are outrageous, humorous, or related to people you know (or all 3!)
> Can be visual, auditory, kinesthetic

List any mnemonics you can think of that would be helpful for Quantitative Reasoning.

```
┌─────────────────────────────────────────────────────────────┐
│                                                             │
│                                                             │
│                                                             │
│                                                             │
└─────────────────────────────────────────────────────────────┘
```

Create a mnemonic to help you remember each of the following.

Order of Operations

Parentheses → Exponents → Multiplication & Division → Addition & Subtraction

```
┌─────────────────────────────────────────────────────────────┐
│                                                             │
│                                                             │
│                                                             │
└─────────────────────────────────────────────────────────────┘
```

Logarithms

$b^e = r \quad \rightarrow \quad \log_b r = e$

Practice

> Spaced repetition
> - To consolidate memory, you must: _____ and _____
> The Quantitative Reasoning section rewards *efficiency*
> - When reviewing questions, challenge yourself to improve your speed
> - Record strategies that improve your efficiency in your LLJ

Rewrite the following word problems as math expressions and solve.

Derek is taller than Laura, who is taller than Jim. Derek is 3 feet taller than Jim, who is half as tall as one foot taller than Laura's height. If the difference between Laura's and Jim's heights is twice the difference between Derek's and Laura's heights, how tall is Jim?

A train is traveling 50 mph directly east while a vehicle is traveling 30 mph directly west. If the train and vehicle are separated by a distance of 100 miles, how long will it take for them to meet?

Bonus: Can you write a word problem described by the following math expression?

$\frac{180x}{4} = 10x + 455$

Practice Cooldown

1. An investment of $1,000,000 carries an interest rate of 0.05 percent quarterly. How much interest will accrue over the next year, rounded to the nearest dollar?
   A. $1999
   B. $2,000
   C. $2,001
   D. $2,002

2. A farmer is building a shed with a slanted roof adjacent to his home, as shown below. Its height will be 7 feet on the side adjacent to the house and 5 feet on the side far from the house, and its width and length have the same dimensions. If the total space inside the shed is 165,888 in³, what is its length in feet?

   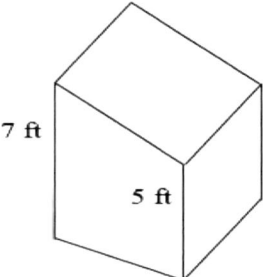

   A. 4
   B. 5
   C. 6
   D. 7

3. In a fictional form of currency, there are 9 hoppies in a lesch, 4 lesches in a doop, and 3 doops in a scran. Dimitri is 14 lesches richer than Lucas, who has 2 more scrans than Dina. How much more currency does Dimitri have than Dina?
   A. 31 lesches
   B. 38 lesches
   C. 6 doops and 14 lesches
   D. 9 doops and 2 lesches

4. Which of the following does not yield an integer?
   A. $\log_2(\frac{1}{2})$
   B. $\log_2(1)$
   C. $\log_2(128)$
   D. $\log_2(144)$

5. Find $\frac{(1.19\times10^{-13})(0.0000062)}{7.50\times10^{-2}}$
    A. 9.84×10^{-16}
    B. 9.84×10^{-18}
    C. 9.84×10^{-20}
    D. 9.84×10^{-22}

To Do After Lesson 6

❏ Full-Length 1
❏ Review Full-Length 1

Critical Reading 2

LESSON 7

To Do Before Lesson 7

- ❏ Complete Full-Length 1
- ❏ Review Full-Length 1

In Lesson 7

- > Question Strategy
- > Question Types
- > Practice Cooldown

To Do After Lesson 7

- ❏ Read Biological Processes Ch. 6–8
- ❏ Complete BP Ch. 6–8 End of Chapter Questions

Question Strategy

1. Translate the Question

> - We will *explicitly* discuss strategies that should become *implicit* by Test Day so you don't have to think about them.
> - Don't worry about classifying questions into their question types—although this can be helpful during practice if certain question types are trickier than others.
> - These strategies are especially helpful for tricky questions—you may answer some straightforward questions easily without extra help.
> - Simply translate the question into what it is *really* asking.

Translate the following questions into what they are* really *asking. The first question has been completed as an example.

1. The author would probably agree with which of the following statements about physiological drives?

    Example: *Which answer choice best fits the author's argument(s) about physiological drives?*

    _____

2. What is the author's purpose in writing, in the final paragraph, that food would take precedence over the other needs listed?

    _____

    _____

    _____

3. An energy-dense drink like soda often meets energy needs far before it provides the person consuming it with a sense of fullness. The passage author would probably consider this:

    _____

    _____

    _____

4. What is the author's purpose in writing, in the second paragraph, that not all physiological needs have been confirmed to be homeostatic?

    _____

    _____

    _____

5. Biologist Ernst Mayr argued that complex biological phenomena generally could not always be broken down to sets of simple, isolated relationships, but would remain intertwined and mathematically inexact. The passage author would likely:

___

___

___

2. Research and Predict an Answer

> - Very often the correct answer can be found in a sentence (or more) within the *same* paragraph as the idea or detail mentioned in the question stem.
> - Research the idea mentioned in the question stem by locating it in the passage.
> - Based on your research and your understanding of the question, make a prediction for what you will be looking for among the answer choices. Then eliminate answer choices that do not fit—this will save time in the long run.
> - The correct answer will most closely mimic the answer suggested by the passage, and at times it will most closely mimic the main idea of that paragraph (or the entire passage).
> - Return to the passage if needed to locate the sites where the remaining answer choices are mentioned and determine whether each fits your predicted answer.

The questions above were associated with the following passage. Find the location of the idea tested by each question, if possible, and make a prediction for each. The first question has been completed as an example.

PRACTICE PASSAGE

The needs that are usually taken as the starting point for motivation theory are the so-called physiological drives. Two recent lines of research make it necessary to revise our customary notions about these needs: first, the development of the concept of homeostasis, and second, the finding that appetites (preferential choices among foods) are a fairly efficient indication of actual needs or lacks in the body.

Thus, it seems impossible as well as useless to make any list of fundamental physiological needs for they can come to almost any number one might wish, depending on the degree of specificity of description. We ==cannot identify all physiological needs as homeostatic==. That sexual desire, sleepiness, sheer activity and maternal behavior in animals, are homeostatic, has not yet been demonstrated. Furthermore, this list would not include the various sensory pleasures (tastes, smells, tickling, stroking) which are probably physiological and which may become the goals of motivated behavior.

In a previous paper, it has been pointed out that these physiological drives or needs are to be considered unusual rather than typical because they are isolable, and because they are localizable somatically. That is to say, they are ==relatively independent== of each other, of other motivations and of the organism as a whole, and secondly, in many cases, it is possible to demonstrate a ==localized, underlying somatic base== for the drive. This is true less generally than has been thought (exceptions are fatigue, sleepiness, maternal responses), but it is still true in the classic instances of hunger, sex, and thirst.

> It should be pointed out again that any of the physiological needs and the consummatory behavior involved with them serve as ==channels for all sorts of other needs== as well. That is to say, the person who thinks he is hungry may actually be seeking more for comfort, or dependence, than for vitamins or proteins. Conversely, it is possible to satisfy the hunger need in part by other activities such as drinking water or smoking cigarettes. In other words, relatively isolable as these physiological needs are, they are not completely so.
>
> Undoubtedly these ==physiological needs are the most pre-potent== of all needs. What this means specifically is, that in the human being who is missing everything in life in an extreme fashion, it is most likely that the major motivation would be the physiological needs rather than any others. A person who is lacking food, safety, love, and esteem would most probably hunger for food more strongly than for anything else.
>
> [Adapted from "A Theory of Human Motivation", *Psychological Review*, by A.H. Maslow, 1943.]

1. The author would probably agree with which of the following statements about physiological drives?

   Example: *The author makes a lot of arguments about physiological drives (as highlighted above), but most likely the answer will say something about physiological drives not all being homeostatic, being independent of one another, having a somatic cause, being channels for other needs, or being pre-potent.*

2. What is the author's purpose in writing, in the final paragraph, that food would take precedence over the other needs listed?

   _____

   _____

   _____

3. An energy-dense drink like soda often meets energy needs far before it provides the person consuming it with a sense of fullness. The passage author would probably consider this:

   _____

   _____

   _____

4. What is the author's purpose in writing, in the second paragraph, that not all physiological needs have been confirmed to be homeostatic?

___

___

___

5. Biologist Ernst Mayr argued that complex biological phenomena generally could not always be broken down to sets of simple, isolated relationships, but would remain intertwined and mathematically inexact. The passage author would likely:

___

___

___

3. Answer the Question

> - If you have not done so already, try to eliminate at least two answer choices.
> - Compare the two remaining answer choices.
> - Identify fatal flaws in either answer choice.
> - Eliminate absolute or extreme answer choices (i.e., *only*, *best*, *never*, etc.) in favor of more flexible terms (i.e., *sometimes*, *may*, *can*, etc.).
> - Find the answer choice that most closely matches the main idea of the passage.
> - Indisputably justify the correct answer with supportive text from the passage.
> - Ensure that the correct answer is accurate *and* addresses the question.
> - *Never* leave a question blank.

Use the recommended question strategies to find the correct answer to each question.

1. The author would probably agree with which of the following statements about physiological drives?
   A. A few of the fundamental physiological needs still need to be identified.
   B. Homeostasis is the result of satisfying a physiological need.
   C. The physiological drives do not form a discrete, clearly-defined category.
   D. The strongest physiological drives refer to those needs which are socially-oriented.

   Example: We can eliminate answer choice D because the last paragraph states that physiological needs take precedence over social needs. Notice that this answer choice also contains an extreme term ("strongest"). We can also eliminate answer choice B because it is contradicted by Paragraph 2, which states that not all physiological needs are homeostatic. Comparing A and C, there is not any information in the passage to support answer choice A. We can prove that answer choice C is correct by identifying the text in Paragraph 3 that says physiological drives are "relatively independent" and "isolable," and the main idea that physiological needs are hard to classify, as suggested in Paragraph 2: "it seems impossible . . . to make any list of fundamental physiological needs for they can come to almost any number one might wish." Answer choice C is correct.

2. What is the author's purpose in writing, in the final paragraph, that food would take precedence over the other needs listed?
   A. To support his argument that urgency and priority are a better definition of physiological needs than homeostasis.
   B. To argue that hunger is a fundamental physiological drive, while love and safety aren't.
   C. To show an example of the non-isolable nature of even the fundamental physiological needs.
   D. To prove that fundamental physiological needs cannot be met by alternate activities.

3. An energy-dense drink like soda often meets energy needs far before it provides the person consuming it with a sense of fullness. The passage author would probably consider this:
   A. an example of the overlapping nature of some physiological needs.
   B. evidence of the non-physiological nature of hunger.
   C. evidence that social training can overcome or confuse physiological drives.
   D. an indication that hunger is non-homeostatic.

4. What is the author's purpose in writing, in the second paragraph, that not all physiological needs have been confirmed to be homeostatic?
   A. To support the inclusion of sensory pleasures to the list of recognized physiological needs.
   B. To introduce the unconfirmed needs, sexual desire, sleepiness, maternal instinct, etc.
   C. To provide evidence that the present definition of physiological needs is problematic.
   D. To provide further evidence against homeostasis as a dominant organizing principle.

5. Biologist Ernst Mayr argued that complex biological phenomena generally could not always be broken down to sets of simple, isolated relationships, but would remain intertwined and mathematically inexact. The passage author would likely:
   A. agree that biological reductionism is a dead end.
   B. admit that perfect isolability is impossible.
   C. acknowledge the difficulty in reductionism, but not its irrelevance.
   D. dismiss the idea that a simple, rule-based understanding can never be achieved.

Solutions:

1. C

2. A

3. A

4. C

5. C

Question Types

> There are only so many ways that questions will be asked, testing a discrete set of skills.
> Do not concern yourself with memorizing or identifying each question category on tests, but recognize when a particular question type is difficult for you and take action.

Write down a strategy that would be helpful for each question type.

Comprehension

QUESTION TYPE	DEFINITION	STRATEGY
Words in Context	defining words as used in the passage	
Main Idea	identifying the main idea of the passage or paragraphs	
Supporting Detail	determining facts or ideas stated in the passage	
Drawing Conclusions	making inferences based on the passage	

Analysis

QUESTION TYPE	DEFINITION	STRATEGY
Relationships Between Ideas	defining relationships between ideas	
Author's Purpose	determining the author's purpose in writing the passage or paragraphs	
Author's Tone	determining the author's opinion	
Facts vs. Opinions	differentiating between facts and opinions	
Rhetorical Strategies	identifying why certain writing methods and phrases were used	

Evaluation

QUESTION TYPE	DEFINITION	STRATEGY
Bias	evaluating the author's position within the passage	
Support in an Argument	determining the effectiveness of the support used by the author	
Author's Conclusion	identifying the author's main thesis	

Practice Cooldown

Speech is so familiar a feature of daily life that we rarely pause to define it. It seems as natural to man as walking, and only less so than breathing. Yet it needs but a moment's reflection to convince us that this naturalness of speech is but an illusory feeling. The process of acquiring speech is, in sober fact, an utterly different sort of thing from the process of learning to walk. The normal human being is predestined to walk, not because his elders will assist him to learn the art, but because his organism is prepared from birth, or even from the moment of conception, to take on all those expenditures of nervous energy and all those muscular adaptations that result in walking.

Not so language. Eliminate society and it is certain that a new-born individual will never learn to talk. Or remove him from the social environment into which he has come and transplant him to an utterly alien one. His speech will be completely at variance with the speech of his native environment.

Interjections are among the least important of speech elements. But their discussion is valuable mainly because it can be shown that even they, avowedly the nearest of all language sounds to instinctive utterance, are only superficially of an instinctive nature. Were it therefore possible to demonstrate that the whole of language is traceable, in its ultimate historical and psychological foundations, to the interjections, it would still not follow that language is an instinctive activity.

But, as a matter of fact, all attempts so to explain the origin of speech have been fruitless. There is no tangible evidence, historical or otherwise, tending to show that the mass of speech elements and speech processes has evolved out of the interjections. These are a very small and functionally insignificant proportion of the vocabulary of language; at no time and in no linguistic province that we have record of do we see a noticeable tendency towards their elaboration into the primary warp and woof of language. They are never more, at best, than a decorative edging to the ample, complex fabric.

The way is now cleared, then, for a serviceable definition of language. Language is a purely human and non-instinctive method of communicating ideas, emotions, and desires by means of a system of voluntarily produced symbols. There is no discernible instinctive basis in human speech as such, and such human or animal communication, if "communication" it may be called, as is brought about by involuntary, instinctive cries is not, in our sense, language at all.

[Adapted from *An Introduction to the Study of Speech*, by Edward Sapir, 1921.]

Main Ideas

1.

2.

3.

4.

5.

Thesis:

1. The author would likely agree with which of the following?
   A. Human language and non-verbal communication have very little overlap.
   B. If interjections were truly instinctive, the possibility of an instinctive component in language could not be completely dismissed.
   C. If raised outside of human society, it is unlikely a child can ever run.
   D. Non-human animals do not possess even the rudiments of language.

2. Which of the following would *weaken* the author's argument about animal communication?
   A. Ant communication can be described as emergent behavior, arising from a series of simple rules, unconsciously followed by individual ants.
   B. Gorillas trained in sign-language will create novel sentences from known words.
   C. Parrots can be trained to carry out simple scripted conversations, learning to give an appropriate response to certain recognized phrases in exchange for a food reward.
   D. Studies show patients with damage to particular parts of the brain sometimes lose the ability to process or use verbs, but not nouns.

3. According to the passage, an individual develops language:
   A. as naturally as walking, and only less so than breathing.
   B. through the slow building up of involuntary cries and learned interjections.
   C. when immersed in a language-using society.
   D. automatically when the brain reaches a certain level of development.

4. During the Turing test, a human communicates with both other humans and a programmed artificial device via text displays only. If the artificial device cannot be reliably distinguished from real humans based on conversation only, it has passed the test. Some argue that passing the Turing test is equivalent to understanding language. Which of the following would the author likely believe?
   A. The machine, because it is taught the rules by humans, can be considered language-using.
   B. A machine can only truly use language if it can pass the Turing test.
   C. A failure of the Turing test does not preclude true language use by a machine if it is sufficiently advanced.
   D. A machine that passes the Turing test is not an example of true language use.

5. According to the passage, which of the following is NOT true of interjections?
   A. They are the only examples of language sounds found to be of instinctive utterance.
   B. They are not significant aspects of language.
   C. There is no evidence that interjections have ever evolved into speech elements or processes.
   D. They are distinct from involuntary animal cries.

To Do After Lesson 7

❏ Read Biological Processes Ch. 6–8
❏ Complete BP Ch. 6–8 End of Chapter Questions

Biological Processes 2

To Do Before Lesson 8

- ❏ Read Biological Processes Ch. 6–8
- ❏ Complete BP Ch. 6–8 End of Chapter Questions

In Lesson 8

> Passage Strategy
> Figure Interpretation
> Practice Cooldown

To Do After Lesson 8

- ❏ Read Chemical Processes Ch. 22–23
- ❏ Complete CP Ch. 22–23 End of Chapter Questions

Passage Strategy

Timing
- You will have _____ minutes to answer _____ questions (~_____ min per question).
- There will be 5–6 science passages, which will generally be short, so avoid skipping or skimming. Each passage will be associated with 4 questions.
- Clock management
  - Be _____, not reactive
  - Check time every ~10 questions
  - Allow time to return to marked questions at the end

Active Reading
- Focus on _____, not complicated strategies.
- Reading passages should be an _____ process. If it is an *informational* passage, make a mental note of the main idea of each paragraph. If it is an *experimental* passage, make a mental note of the:
  - Purpose or hypothesis
  - Methods
  - Results
  - Figures
- **Avoid** note-taking or skipping passages as these are time-consuming and provide little or no benefit. The only exception to note-taking is: _____
- Reflect periodically to ensure that you understand whether the results support or address the hypothesis and how the methods relate to the results.

Interpret the purpose, methods, and results in the experimental passage below.

MITOTIC DIVISION

Immediately after fertilization, the human embryo undergoes rapid and drastic changes. These changes are largely driven by mitosis, the process through which cells replicate their chromosomes and divide. Mitosis is broken into four main steps: prophase, metaphase, anaphase, and telophase. During prophase, cells condense their chromosomes and begin to form the mitotic spindles used to separate the chromosomes evenly into the two daughter cells. During metaphase, the chromosomes align along the metaphase plate and begin to be pulled apart by the mitotic spindles. In anaphase, the chromosomes are separated, forming two identical sister chromatids, and are pulled to opposite ends of the dividing cell. Finally, in telophase, the two daughter cells pull apart followed by the formation of a new nucleus in each cell. Both daughter cells are genetically identical to the original cell. This cascade of events occurs in all body cells, including germ cells.

Cancer cells are known for unregulated, continuous mitotic division. A cancer researcher performs an experiment testing the effects of various chemotherapy molecules on two cancer cell lines. The first chemotherapeutic she tests is docetaxel, a mitotic inhibitor that binds reversibly to microtubules. The second inhibitor she tests is ibrutinib, an inhibitor of Bruton's tyrosine kinase (BTK), an enzyme involved in B cell development. The doubling times for the two inhibitors with both cell lines are provided in Table 1.

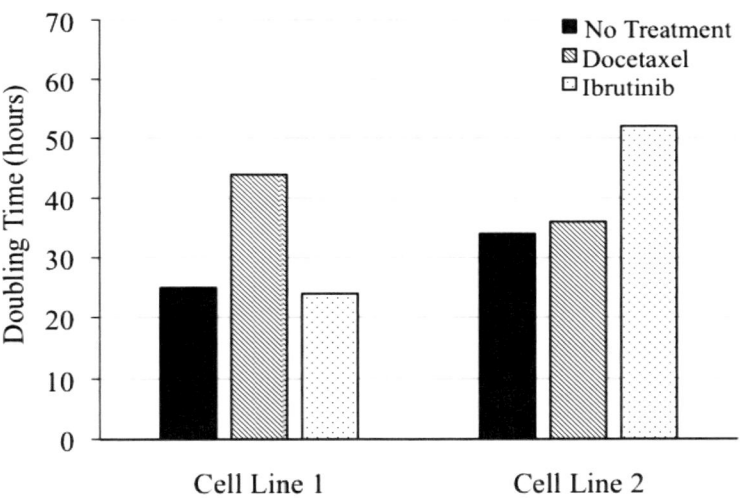

Figure 1. Doubling times for the two inhibitors with both cell lines.

Purpose:

Methods:

Results:

Panic Mode

> With only a few minutes remaining, skim passages by reading the first and last sentence of each paragraph, focusing on the results and briefly examining the figure(s) before answering the questions.

Practice the Panic Mode approach by reading the passage below in 1 minute.

HEME METABOLISM

The first step in the metabolism of heme released from degraded red blood cells is its oxidation by the microsomal enzyme heme oxygenase, resulting in the green pigment biliverdin. The next step is the reduction of biliverdin to a yellow tetrapyrol pigment called bilirubin. This "unconjugated" bilirubin is bound to albumin and transported through the bloodstream to the liver. In the liver, it is conjugated with glucuronic acid by the enzyme glucuronyl transferase, forming bilirubin diglucuronide—"conjugated bilirubin." From the liver, this solubilized form of bilirubin is excreted, initially as part of bile, and eventually, from the body.

In neonates, benign "physiological" jaundice is of least concern clinically, and tends to develop after the first 24 hours of life due to an accumulation of unconjugated bilirubin in the blood (hyperbilirubinemia). This leads to the symptoms of jaundice, including a pronounced yellowing of the skin and sclera. Alternatively, neonatal jaundice may be of greater concern if a pathological condition is responsible for an elevation of bilirubin. Severe hyperbilirubinemia, especially elevation of conjugated bilirubin, may cause accumulation of bilirubin in the brain leading to irreversible neurological damage—a condition referred to as kernicterus.

A pediatrician evaluating the cases of two newborns made the observations recorded below (Note: In infants, normal total serum bilirubin < 12 mg/dL, conjugated bilirubin < 2 mg/dL, and unconjugated bilirubin < 10 mg/dL).

Case 1
A 3-day-old male infant born exhibiting yellow discoloration of the skin, most notably of the forehead and neck.

Case 2
A 2-week-old, healthy female infant is slightly jaundiced. Labs show a total bilirubin of 18 mg/dL and a conjugated bilirubin of 0.8 mg/dL.

Main Ideas

1.

2.

3.

4.

5.

Results Interpretation:

LESSON 8: BIOLOGICAL PROCESSES 2

Figure Interpretation

> Read the caption to understand the purpose of the figure.
> Examine the axes and identify which is altered (the _____ variable, usually found on the _____-axis) and which is being measured (the _____ variable, usually found on the _____-axis).
> Identify the main effect(s) of each variable that is changed by comparing to the control.
> Don't spend too much time here—especially on molecular structures, pathways, or reactions.

Decode the figures presented below.

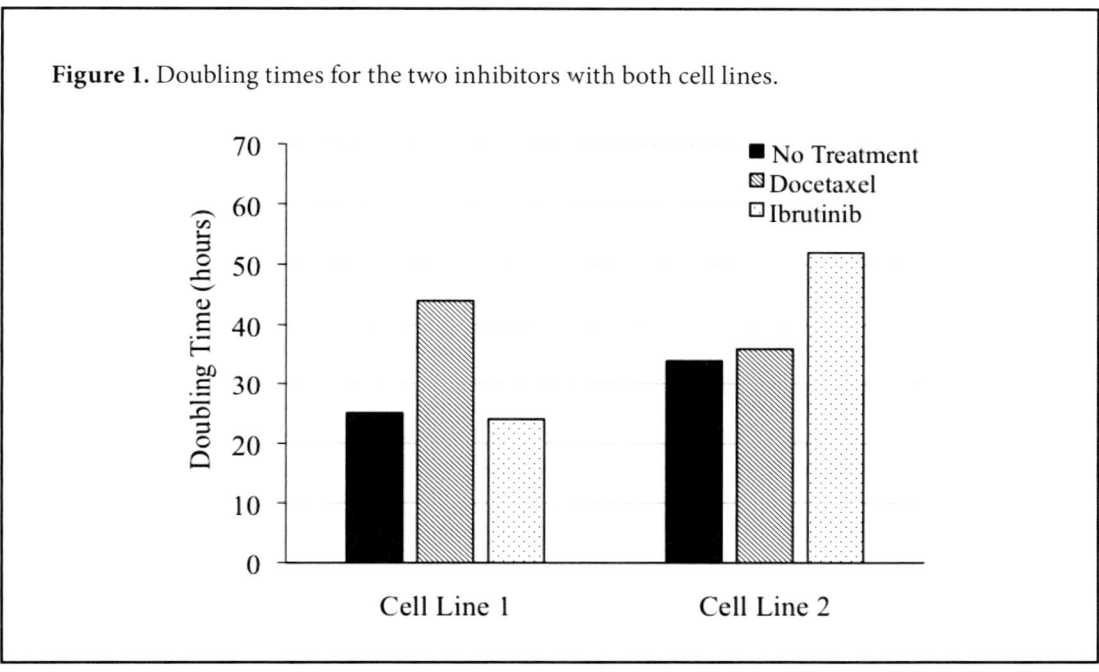

Figure 1. Doubling times for the two inhibitors with both cell lines.

1. What is the purpose of this figure?

   _____

   _____

2. The independent variables are: _____

   The dependent variable is: _____

3. What are the main effects of each independent variable?

   a. _____

   _____

   b. _____

   _____

4. What is the significance of the results shown in this table?

   _____

   _____

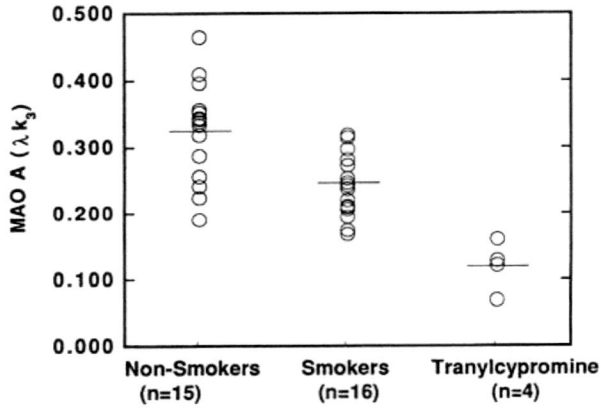

Figure 2. Comparison of MAO A levels in the thalamus as expressed by the model term $\lambda k3$ for nonsmokers (n = 15), smokers (n = 16), and nonsmokers treated with tranylcypromine (n = 4).

Image adapted from: Fowler et al., 1996. Brain monoamine oxidase A inhibition in cigarette smokers. PNAS 93(24), 14065-9.

1. What is the purpose of this figure?

   _____

   _____

LESSON 8: BIOLOGICAL PROCESSES 2

2. The independent variables are: _____

   The dependent variable is: _____

3. What are the main effects of each independent variable?

   a. _____
   _____

   b. _____
   _____

4. What is the significance of the results shown in this figure?
   _____
   _____

Table 1. Classification of the trinucleotide repeat on an HTT allele and resulting Huntington disease status.

REPEAT COUNT	DISEASE STATUS	AGE OF ONSET	PROBABILITY OF AFFECTED OFFSPRING
<26	Will not be affected	N/A	None
27-35	Will not be affected	N/A	Elevated but <50%
36-39	May be affected	After 40	50%
40+	Will be affected	Ages 25–39; earlier with increased repeat count	50%

1. What is the purpose of this table?
   _____
   _____

2. The correlational variables are: _____
   _____

3. What are the main effects?

   a.

4. What is the significance of the results shown in this table?

Practice Cooldown

1. DNA replication is understood to be semiconservative. To demonstrate this, a geneticist radiolabeled a fragment of dsDNA and allowed it to replicate. After three successive replication cycles, what fraction of the total DNA consists of the original parent material?
   A. $\frac{1}{4}$
   B. $\frac{1}{8}$
   C. $\frac{1}{16}$
   D. $\frac{1}{32}$

2. The structure of a typical nucleoside includes:
   A. six-carbon sugar.
   B. a nitrogenous base.
   C. phosphate groups.
   D. A and B only.

3. Part of the replication fork on a eukaryotic dsDNA molecule is shown below. At which point does the lagging strand of the new DNA molecule begin to form?

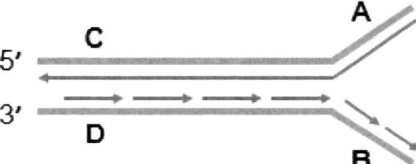

   A. A
   B. B
   C. C
   D. D

4. How does the initiation step of transcription differ from that of DNA replication?
   A. Replication involves a DNA-dependent DNA polymerase, while transcription utilizes an RNA-dependent RNA polymerase.
   B. DNA replication is semiconservative and utilizes Okazaki fragments, while transcription forms a single-stranded product.
   C. Only DNA replication begins at particular points in the DNA known as origins.
   D. The processes do not differ notably; both transcription and replication require RNA primers due to the free -OH groups at their 3' ends.

5. The sense strand of the DNA corresponding to a typical membrane-bound protein contains the segment 5'-TTTTTCGTG-3'. From the N to the C terminus, the associated protein sequence is:
   A. phenylalanine, leucine, valine.
   B. valine, phenylalanine, phenylalanine.
   C. histidine, glutamic acid, lysine.
   D. phenylalanine, phenylalanine, valine.

6. Twenty standard amino acids are found in typical human proteins. How many unique mRNA codons exist?
   A. 16
   B. 20
   C. 32
   D. 64

7. The wild-type and mutated forms of an mRNA transcript are shown below. What kind of mutation occurred?

   WT: 5'-CAUUAUGACCGGAGU-3'
   Mut: 5'-CAUUACUGACCGGGAGU-3'

   A. Frameshift
   B. Substitution
   C. Silent
   D. Nonsense

8. Red hair is recessive to all other hair colors. If the incidence of red-headed individuals within a certain population is only 9%, what percent of that population are heterozygous for the "red hair" allele?
   A. 16%
   B. 21%
   C. 30%
   D. 42%

9. A rare type of orchid faces a unique challenge to find adequate sunlight. Plants that are too small are covered by undergrowth, while plants that reach too high are preyed upon by grazing herbivores. Over time, these orchids have, on average, grown to vary only slightly in height. This situation exemplifies which type of selection?
   A. Speciation
   B. Stabilizing selection
   C. Directional selection
   D. Disruptive selection

10. A flower displaying the dominant trait (long stem, L) is crossed with a flower displaying the recessive trait (short stem, l). Half of the offspring produced have long stems and half have short stems. The genotypes of the parent flowers must have been:
    A. Ll and ll
    B. LL and ll
    C. LL and LL
    D. Ll and Ll

To Do After Lesson 8

- ❑ Read Chemical Processes Ch. 22–23
- ❑ Complete CP Ch. 22–23 End of Chapter Questions

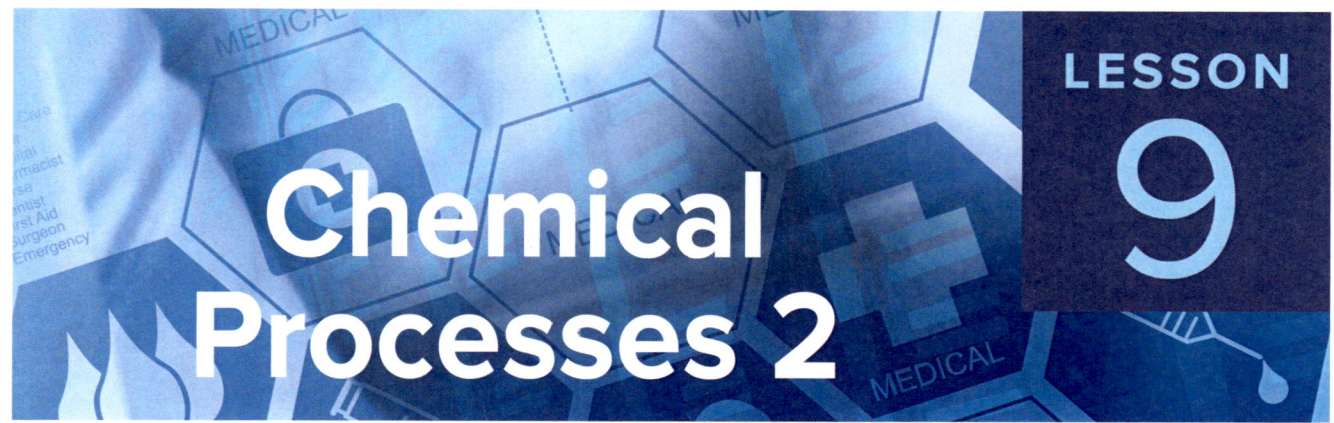

Chemical Processes 2

To Do Before Lesson 9

- ❑ Read Chemical Processes Ch. 22–23
- ❑ Complete CP Ch. 22–23 End of Chapter Questions

In Lesson 9

> Passage Strategy
> Passage Practice
> Practice Cooldown

To Do After Lesson 9

- ❑ Read Quantitative Reasoning Ch. 30–31
- ❑ Complete QR Ch. 30–31 End of Chapter Questions

Passage Strategy

Strategy Recap

> You will have _____ minutes to answer _____ questions (~_____ min per question).
> Be _____ about timing, not reactive.
> Focus on _____, not complicated strategies.
> If it is an *informational* passage, make a mental note of the main idea of each paragraph. If it is an *experimental* passage, make a mental note of the:
  - Purpose or hypothesis
    - Methods
    - Results
    - Figures
> **Avoid** note-taking except when: _____
> Reflect periodically

Figures and Tables

> Read the caption and examine the axes to determine the independent and dependent variables
> Identify the main effect(s) of each independent variable
> Briefly glance at molecular structures, reactions, and pathways

LESSON 9: CHEMICAL PROCESSES 2

Identify the purpose, methods, results, and figure in the experimental passage below.

POLYPEPTIDES

The structure of a polypeptide was determined beginning with the identification of its constituent amino acids. A purified sample of the polypeptide was denatured and then hydrolyzed by a strong acid at 110°C for 24 hours. The individual amino acids released by the treatment were then separated by cation-exchange chromatography. In this technique, amino acids bind with differing affinities to negatively-charged groups attached to resins along the column.

Following treatment with a series of eluting solutions, the separated amino acids in the eluate were heated with ninhydrin—a reagent that forms the blue-purple compound Ruhemann's Purple with most amino acids, amines, and ammonia.

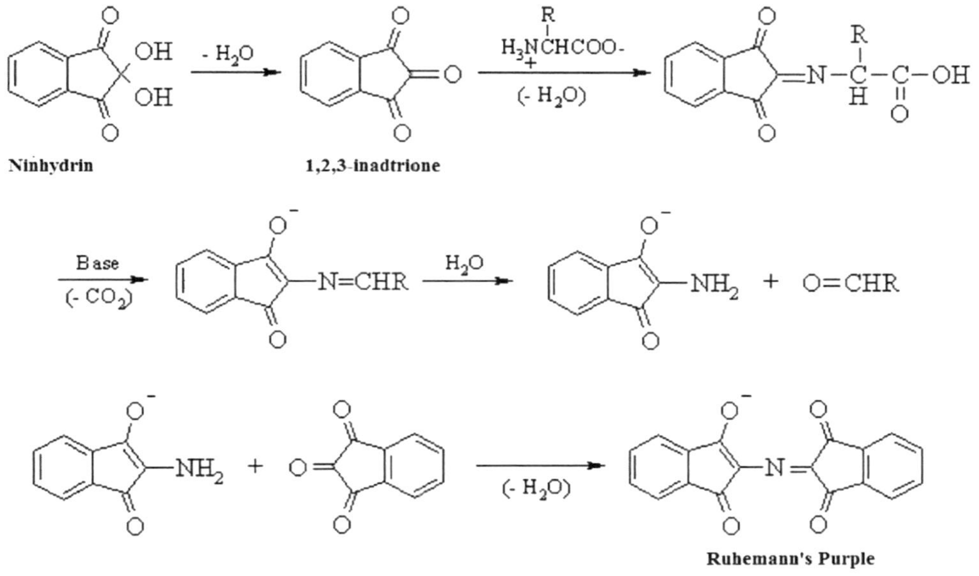

Figure 1. The ninhydrin reaction between ninhydrin and a free amino acid.

The amount of each amino acid present was then determined spectrophotometrically by measuring the amount of blue-purple light absorbed.

The specific position of each amino acid in the polypeptide chain was also determined. Edman reagent (phenylisothiocyanate) was used to label a terminal residue under mildly alkaline conditions, resulting in the formation of a phenylthiocarbamoyl. Under acidic conditions, the terminal amino acid of the polypeptide was cleaved, releasing free polypeptide and phenylthiohydantoin (PTH), an amino acid derivative. Edman reagent was applied repeatedly, shortening the peptide bond obtained following each cycle. The steps of the Edman degradation are shown in Figure 2.

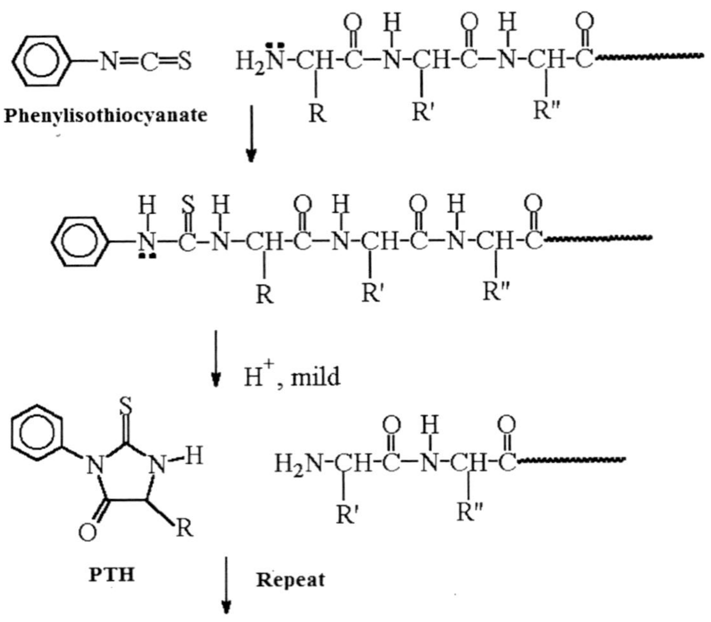

Figure 2. Edman degradation of a polypeptide.

There are limits on the length of polypeptides that can be sequenced by this method. Over time, the yield of PTH-amino acid products decreases relative to the background level of PTH-amino acids. Repetitive yield is a measure of the percent of detectable material remaining after each turn of the cycle. Longer polypeptides can be sequenced from greater initial sample sizes and larger repetitive yields. They may also be cleaved by peptidase enzymes to create shorter polypeptides for sequencing.

Purpose:

Methods:

Results:

Figures:

Panic Mode

> With only a few minutes remaining, skim passages by reading the first and last sentence of each paragraph before quickly answering the questions.

Practice the Panic Mode approach by reading the passage below in 2 minutes.

KIDNEY STONES

Kidney stones are insoluble aggregate crystals that can form in the urine of certain people. One of the compounds that can contribute to the formation of kidney stones is calcium oxalate (CaC_2O_4, FW = 128.097 g/mol, K_{sp} = 2.3 x 10^{-9}). Oxalic acid is a naturally occurring diprotic acid, ($H_2C_2O_4$, pK_{a1} = 1.3 and pK_{a2} = 4.3) present in a number of foods, including rhubarb and spinach. Oxalic acid can be produced from oxaloacetate, which plays an important role in the citric acid cycle. Uric acid can also contribute to the formation of kidney stones and can crystallize in the synovial fluid of joints, producing inflammation and the painful symptoms associated with gout. In humans, uric acid is the final oxidation product of purine metabolism and, like oxalic acid, is a diprotic acid ($H_2C_5H_2N_4O_3$, pK_{a1} = 5.4 and pK_{a2} = 10.3), but unlike oxalic acid, it is not completely ionized at pH levels typical for urine.

If the urine becomes supersaturated, seed crystals can result in the formation of a large mass, or stone, in one of several locations, such as the bladder, ureters, or kidneys. In many cases, small stones (< 3 mm) are readily passed. However, large stones can cause obstruction and renal colic. In some cases, ultrasound can be used to break up stones and facilitate their passing, but in extreme cases, surgery may be required.

Urine contains natural chelating agents, one of which is citrate. These chelating agents are polydentate ligands (Lewis bases) that coordinate to a metal ion and form soluble coordination compounds that help prevent the nucleation and precipitation of calcium oxalate. Citric acid is a weak triprotic acid (pK_{a1} = 3.1, pK_{a2} = 4.8, and pK_{a3} = 6.4), whose structure is shown in Figure 1. The equilibrium constant at 37°C for the formation of the calcium citrate complex ion is 1.9 x 10^3 (Reaction 1). The calcium citrate complex has a residual negative charge that enhances its solubility in aqueous solution.

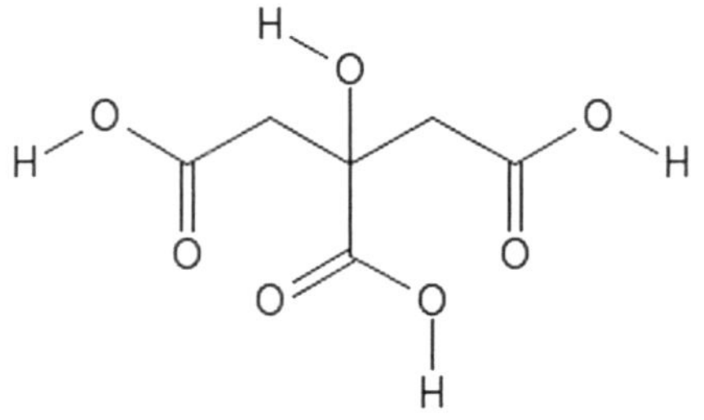

Figure 1. The structure of citric acid, $H_3C_6H_5O_7$. Image adapted from Ugen64 under CC BY-SA 3.0.
Reaction 1. Ca^{2+} (aq) + $C_6H_5O_7^{3-}$ (aq) → $CaC_6H_5O_7^{-}$ (aq)

Main Ideas

1.

2.

3.

Figure:

Reaction:

Passage Practice

Timed Practice

> - Use **timed** practice to: _____
> - Start with one passage at a time, then build to a full Section Test
> - Troubleshoot your optimal pacing by practicing multiple strategies:
>   - <u>Speed Read</u>: 1 min reading + 5 min answering questions
>   - <u>Even-Split</u>: 2–3 min reading + 3 min answering questions
>   - <u>Passage Mastery</u>: 4 min reading + 2 min answering questions

Untimed Practice

> - Use **untimed** practice to: _____
> - Set at least one discrete, actionable goal per untimed practice session

When can you commit to practicing science passages? Daily? Once a week?

What are three goals or skills you would like to improve on science passages?

Review and Analysis

> - Investigate **broad patterns or trends** and develop **actionable goals**.
> - Keep track of trends in your performance over time in your LLJ.

Analyze your performance on the Biological Processes and Chemical Processes passages in Full-Length 1 and answer the following questions in your LLJ.

- Did I feel rushed or run out of time? If so, how can I improve my efficiency?
- Did I make any mistakes? Why did I make those mistakes?
- What strategies did I apply? Did they work?
- What strategies would I like to try?
- Did I return to the passage while answering questions? Did that help?
- Did I skip any passages or questions? Did I leave any questions unanswered?
- Were some passages harder than others? Did I answer a disproportionate number of questions incorrectly on certain passages?
- Which were harder: passage-associated questions or discrete questions? Why?
- Were there any types of questions that I answered incorrectly more than other types of questions?
- For each question I missed, why did I select the incorrect answer?
- For each question I missed, can I point to evidence in the passage text that leads to the correct answer?

Practice Cooldown

1. The heat of vaporization of water is 2256 kJ/kg, while the heat of fusion is 334 kJ/kg. What amount of heat is required to completely transform 80 mL of distilled water at 100 °C into steam, also at 100 °C?
   A. 0 J, since ΔT for this transition is 0
   B. 180 J
   C. 2.7×10^4 J
   D. 1.8×10^5 J

2. Of the following processes, which does not require the input of energy in the form of heat?
   A. A block of ice at -10°C and 1 atm forming a pool of water at 15°C and 1 atm
   B. A beaker of water at 100°C and 1 atm transitioning into steam at 100°C and 1 atm
   C. A block of ice at 230 K and 10 Pa transitioning into water vapor at 50 Pa
   D. A balloon filled with steam at 395 K transitioning into water at 350 K

3. A student wants to transform 100 g of ice at −5°C into water at 15°C. If he does so under standard conditions, how much heat will the entire process require? Note that c_{ice} = 2.03 $\frac{J}{g°C}$, c_{water} = 4.18 $\frac{J}{g°C}$, and H_{fusion} = 334 $\frac{J}{g}$.
   A. 7285 J
   B. 7619 J
   C. 38535 J
   D. 40685 J

4. At STP, a number of moles of argon gas has a volume of 67.2 L. If the approximate molar masses of argon and krypton are 39.95 g/mol and 84.8 g/mol, respectively, what volume will the same number of moles of Kr gas occupy at STP?
   A. 22.4 L
   B. 33.1 L
   C. 67.2 L
   D. 135 L

5. 20 moles of gaseous ammonia are held in a flexible balloon. Under which conditions should this gas behave LEAST ideally?
   A. P = 1×10^5 Pa and T = 298 K
   B. P = 1×10^2 GPa and T = 25 K
   C. P = 25 kPa and T = 800 K
   D. P = 1×10^7 Pa and T = 400 K

6. Two moles of oxygen gas are sequestered in a 3 L container at 1 atm and 15°C. For the temperature of this gas to increase to 83°C, what increase in pressure is necessary? Assume that the volume of the container cannot change.
   A. The pressure must be changed to 1.25 atm.
   B. The pressure must be changed to 2 atm.
   C. The pressure must be changed to 2.5 atm.
   D. The pressure should be increased to 5.5 atm.

7. 17.1 grams of sucrose are added to 10 g of water (K_f = 1.86 °C/m). The freezing point of the water is then measured at -9.3°C. The molecular weight of sucrose is closest to:
   A. 34.2 g/mol.
   B. 85.5 g/mol.
   C. 171 g/mol.
   D. 342 g/mol.

8. Osmotic pressure can be calculated using the formula π = iMRT. If π is given units of atmospheres (atm), what are the units for R?

   A. $\frac{\text{kg atm}}{\text{mol K}}$

   B. $\frac{\text{L atm}}{\text{mol K}}$

   C. $\frac{\text{mol K}}{\text{L atm}}$

   D. R is unitless.

9. A scientist wishes to set up a buffer at a pH of 4.80. Of the following acids, the scientist should use:
   A. hydrofluoric acid ($K_a = 7.2 \times 10^{-4}$).
   B. benzoic acid ($K_a = 6.3 \times 10^{-5}$).
   C. acetic acid ($K_a = 1.8 \times 10^{-5}$).
   D. hydrocyanic acid ($K_a = 6.2 \times 10^{-10}$).

10. 10 ml of a 1.0 M hydrochloric acid solution is added to a 100 mL flask. Next, 90 mL of distilled water is added to the flask, bringing the total volume to 100 mL. What is the pH of the final solution?
    A. 0
    B. 1
    C. 2
    D. 10

To Do After Lesson 9

- ❏ Read Quantitative Reasoning Ch. 30–31
- ❏ Complete QR Ch. 30–31 End of Chapter Questions

Quantitative Reasoning 2

LESSON 10

To Do Before Lesson 10

- ❏ Read Quantitative Reasoning Ch. 30–31
- ❏ Complete QR Ch. 30–31 End of Chapter Questions

In Lesson 10

- > Question Strategy
- > A Word on Word Problems
- > Practice Cooldown

To Do After Lesson 10

- ❏ Read Biological Processes Ch. 9–11
- ❏ Complete BP Ch. 9–11 End of Chapter Questions

Question Strategy

Timing

> - You will have _____ minutes to answer _____ questions (~_____ min per question).
> - Approximately _____ of questions will be word problems.
> - Use Section Tests to gauge and optimize your timing.
> - Efficiency is *critical* on the Quantitative Reasoning section.
>   - Use elimination and estimation where possible.
>   - Familiarize yourself with the standard online calculator provided, and use it to your advantage.
>   - Make an educated guess on particularly laborious or difficult questions (e.g., calculus questions), mark them, and move on. Limit skipped questions to <10. *Easy questions are worth as much as hard questions.*
> - Identify the types of Quantitative Reasoning problems that are most difficult for you and work on them during focused practice sessions. Keep track of strategies that are especially effective for those problem types in your LLJ.

What types of Quantitative Reasoning problems are most difficult for you?

| |
| |
| |

Strategy Development

1. Decide whether to solve or make an educated guess.

2. Set up the appropriate equation(s).

3. Identify the most efficient way to solve and look for shortcuts.

    a. Calculator

    b. Elimination

    c. Estimation

    d. Solving backwards

    e. Plug-and-chug

    f. Substitution

4. Solve.

5. Check your answer—*only* if you have time.

LESSON 10: QUANTITATIVE REASONING 2

Solve the following problems using Quantitative Reasoning Strategies.

1. Solve for y in terms of x: $2x^2-3y=4x^2-\frac{y}{2}$.
   A. $-\frac{4x^2}{5}$
   B. $\frac{4x^2}{5}$
   C. $-\frac{5x^2}{4}$
   D. $\frac{5x^2}{4}$

Solution:

This algebra problem is not too difficult, so let's tackle it right away. The equation we need to use is provided, and we know that we need to use algebraic methods to simplify this polynomial expression and isolate y. We *cannot* use a calculator to solve. Let's start by isolating y terms on one side of the equation and x terms on the other:

$$2x^2-3y = 4x^2-\frac{y}{2}$$

$$\frac{y}{2}-3y = 4x^2-2x^2$$

How can we simplify further? The x terms are like terms, so we can combine them. We need to rewrite the y terms to share a common denominator:

$$\frac{y}{2}-\frac{6y}{2} = 2x^2$$

$$-\frac{5y}{2} = 2x^2$$

To isolate y, we should multiply both sides by the reciprocal of its coefficient ($-\frac{2}{5}$):

$$y = -\frac{4x^2}{5}$$

We feel confident in this answer, and it would take too much time to check our work, so let's move on.

2. Solve $(6x - 4)(x + 2) = 6x^2$ for x.
   A. 1
   B. 2
   C. 3
   D. 4

NextStepTESTPREP.com

Solution:

This is a(n) _____ problem, and I __will / will not__ tackle it right away.

The appropriate equation(s) to use is/are: _____

This problem __can / cannot__ be solved using a calculator.

Are there any shortcuts I can use? _____

I will solve by: _____

Show your work:

---

3. What are the domain and range of the function $f(x) = \frac{1}{x+4}$?
   A. Domain: $x \in R \mid x \neq -4$}; range: $y \in R \mid x \neq 0$}
   B. Domain: $x \in R \mid x \neq 0$}; range: $y \in R \mid x \neq -4$}
   C. Domain: $y \in R \mid y \neq -4$}; range: $x \in R \mid x \neq -4$}
   D. Domain: $y \in R \mid y \neq 0$; range: $x \in R \mid x \neq -0$}

LESSON 10: QUANTITATIVE REASONING 2

Solution:

This is a(n) _____ problem, and I __will / will not__ tackle it right away.

The appropriate equation(s) to use is/are: _____

This problem __can / cannot__ be solved using a calculator.

Are there any shortcuts I can use? _____

I will solve by: _____

Show your work:

4. Jenny drives 8 miles north from her home and then 5 miles west. Then she travels $2\sqrt{2}$ miles in the northeast direction at a 45° angle. If she were to drive in a straight line back to her home, how far would her destination be from her home?
   A. 3.9 mi
   B. 5.2 mi
   C. 7.8 mi
   D. 10.4 mi

Solution:

This is a(n) _____ problem, and I __will / will not__ tackle it right away.

The appropriate equation(s) to use is/are: _____

This problem __can / cannot__ be solved using a calculator.

Are there any shortcuts I can use? _____

I will solve by: _____

Show your work:

A Word on Word Problems

Rewrite the following word problems as math expressions and solve.

A restaurant has a patio seating section and an indoor seating section which has twice as many tables. If the ratio of full tables to empty tables is 1:2 on the patio and 3:1 in the indoor section, what is the ratio of full tables to empty tables for the entire restaurant?

Bill is fishing and catches fish with lengths of 23 in, 17 in, 15 in, and 18 in. How big does his next fish need to be if he wants the average size of the fish he catches to be 20 in?

Bonus: Can you write a word problem described by the following math expressions?

$$12-3x=4y \qquad x+2y=10$$

Practice Cooldown

1. Factor the expression $-6x^2+18x+24$.
   A. $6(x+1)(4-x)$
   B. $6(x-1)(x+4)$
   C. $6(x+1)(x+4)$
   D. $6(x-1)(4-x)$

2. Which of the following logarithms is NOT equivalent to the rest?
   A. log 14x −3 log y
   B. log 14x−log y^3
   C. Log (14x −3y)
   D. log $\frac{14x}{y^3}$

3. If there is a 3% chance of getting accepted into University X, and already 6 of the 352 graduating seniors at Jonathan's high school have been accepted into University X, what is the probability of Jonathan being accepted there based on random chance?
   A. 0.05%
   B. 1.3%
   C. 1.7%
   D. 3.0%

4. Suppose a class takes an exam, and the mean score is 70%, with a standard deviation of 8%. If a student then takes a make-up test and scores a 30%, which statistical parameter is likely to be affected the most?
   A. mode
   B. median
   C. mean
   D. All three will be equally affected.

5. Identify the equation that describes the graph shown below.

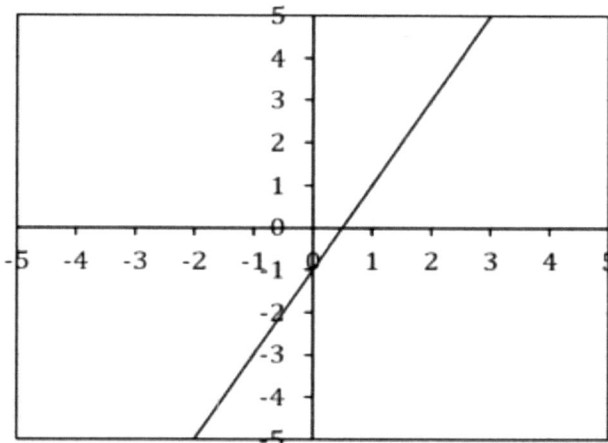

A. $y = \frac{1}{2}x - 1$
B. $y = 2x + \frac{1}{2}$
C. $y = 2x - 1$
D. $y = 2x + 1$

To Do After Lesson 10

❏ Read Biological Processes Ch. 9–11
❏ Complete BP Ch. 9–11 End of Chapter Questions

This page left intentionally blank.

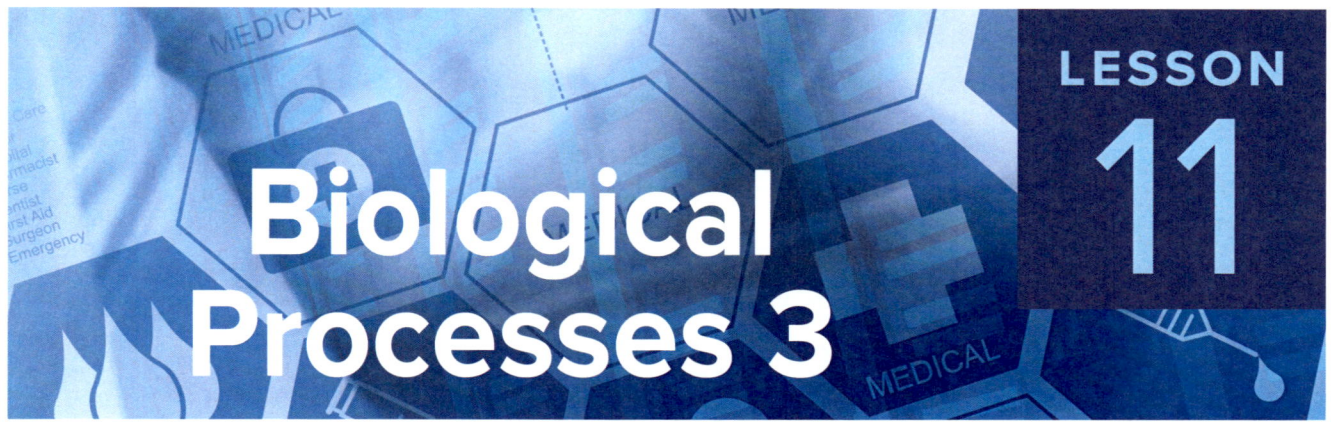

Biological Processes 3

To Do Before Lesson 11

- ❏ Read Biological Processes Ch. 9–11
- ❏ Complete BP Ch. 9–11 End of Chapter Questions

In Lesson 11

- › Science Reasoning Question Strategy
- › Science Recall Question Strategy
- › Practice Cooldown

To Do After Lesson 11

- ❏ Read Chemical Processes Ch. 24–25
- ❏ Complete CP Ch. 24–25 End of Chapter Questions

Science Reasoning Question Strategy

> Science Reasoning is tested on questions associated with passages and requires you to apply your content knowledge to new information.

Translate the Question

> We will *explicitly* discuss strategies that should become *implicit* by Test Day.
> Don't worry about classifying questions into their question types—although this can be helpful during practice if certain question types are trickier than others.
> Simply translate the question into what it is *really* asking.
>   – What content topic or equation is the question addressing?
>   – What passage information is being tested?
> Be vigilant with "except" or "not" question by rephrasing in a way that makes sense to you.

Re-read the passage below (from Lesson 8) and translate the following questions associated with this passage into what they are really asking.

MITOTIC DIVISION

Immediately after fertilization, the human embryo undergoes rapid and drastic changes. These changes are largely driven by mitosis, the process through which cells replicate their chromosomes and divide. Mitosis is broken into four main steps: prophase, metaphase, anaphase, and telophase. During prophase, cells condense their chromosomes and begin to form the mitotic spindles used to separate the chromosomes evenly into the two daughter cells. During metaphase, the chromosomes align along the metaphase plate and begin to be pulled apart by the mitotic spindles. In anaphase, the chromosomes are separated, forming two identical sister chromatids, and are pulled to opposite ends of the dividing cell. Finally, in telophase, the two daughter cells pull apart followed by the formation of a new nucleus in each cell. Both daughter cells are genetically identical to the original cell. This cascade of events occurs in all body cells, including germ cells.

Cancer cells are known for unregulated, continuous mitotic division. A cancer researcher performs an experiment testing the effects of various chemotherapy molecules on two cancer cell lines. The first chemotherapeutic tested is docetaxel, a mitotic inhibitor that binds reversibly to microtubules. The second inhibitor tested is ibrutinib, an inhibitor of Bruton's tyrosine kinase (BTK), an enzyme involved in B cell development. The doubling times for the two inhibitors with both cell lines are provided in Table 1.

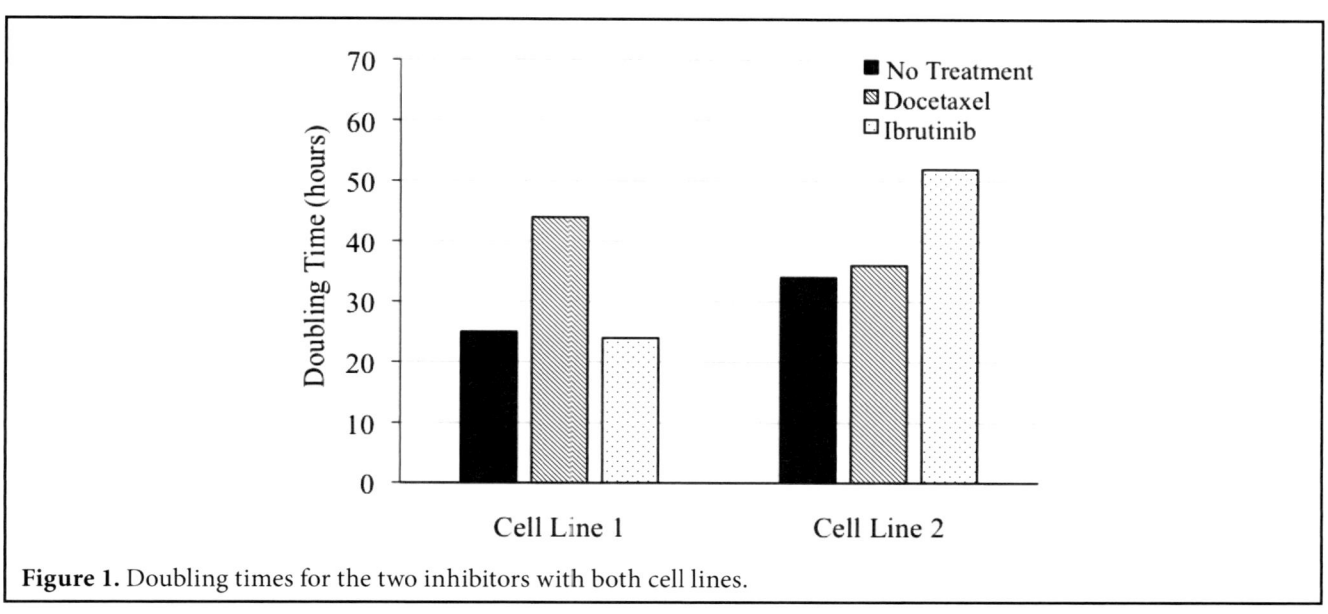

Figure 1. Doubling times for the two inhibitors with both cell lines.

1. Chromosomal crossover, or the exchange of genetic information between homologous chromosomes, occurs in which stage of mitosis?

   Example: *When does crossover occur during mitosis? Answering this question requires content knowledge about cell division. The passage reminds us of the stages of mitosis but does not discuss crossover.*

2. Among non-cancerous cells in the human body, which cells are likely to undergo mitosis at the fastest rate?

3. The restriction point, or the point at which a cell is committed to undergoing mitosis, is located in which stage of interphase?

4. If the researcher examines Cell Line 1 in the presence of docetaxel under a microscope, would the majority be in interphase or a mitotic phase?

_____

_____

_____

5. Research and Predict an Answer
   - What information do you need to answer this question?
     a. Content knowledge? Equations?
     b. Passage information?
     c. Both?
   - Research the idea mentioned in the question stem by locating it in the passage.
   - Based on your research and your understanding of the question, make a prediction for what you will be looking for among the answer choices. Then eliminate answer choices that do not fit—this will save time in the long run.
   - Return to the passage if needed to locate the sites where the remaining answer choices are mentioned and determine whether each fits your predicted answer.
   - Understanding the figures and results of experimental passages is key!

Find the location of the idea tested by each question in the passage, if possible, and make a prediction for each.

MITOTIC DIVISION

Immediately after fertilization, the human embryo undergoes rapid and drastic changes. These changes are largely driven by mitosis, the process through which cells replicate their chromosomes and divide. Mitosis is broken into four main steps: prophase, metaphase, anaphase, and telophase. During prophase, cells condense their chromosomes and begin to form the mitotic spindles used to separate the chromosomes evenly into the two daughter cells. During metaphase, the chromosomes align along the metaphase plate and begin to be pulled apart by the mitotic spindles. In anaphase, the chromosomes are separated, forming two identical sister chromatids, and are pulled to opposite ends of the dividing cell. Finally, in telophase, the two daughter cells pull apart followed by the formation of a new nucleus in each cell. Both daughter cells are genetically identical to the original cell. This cascade of events occurs in all body cells, including germ cells.

Cancer cells are known for unregulated, continuous mitotic division. A cancer researcher performs an experiment testing the effects of various chemotherapy molecules on two cancer cell lines. The first chemotherapeutic tested is docetaxel, a mitotic inhibitor that binds reversibly to microtubules. The second inhibitor tested is ibrutinib, an inhibitor of Bruton's tyrosine kinase (BTK), an enzyme involved in B cell development. The doubling times for the two inhibitors with both cell lines are provided in Table 1.

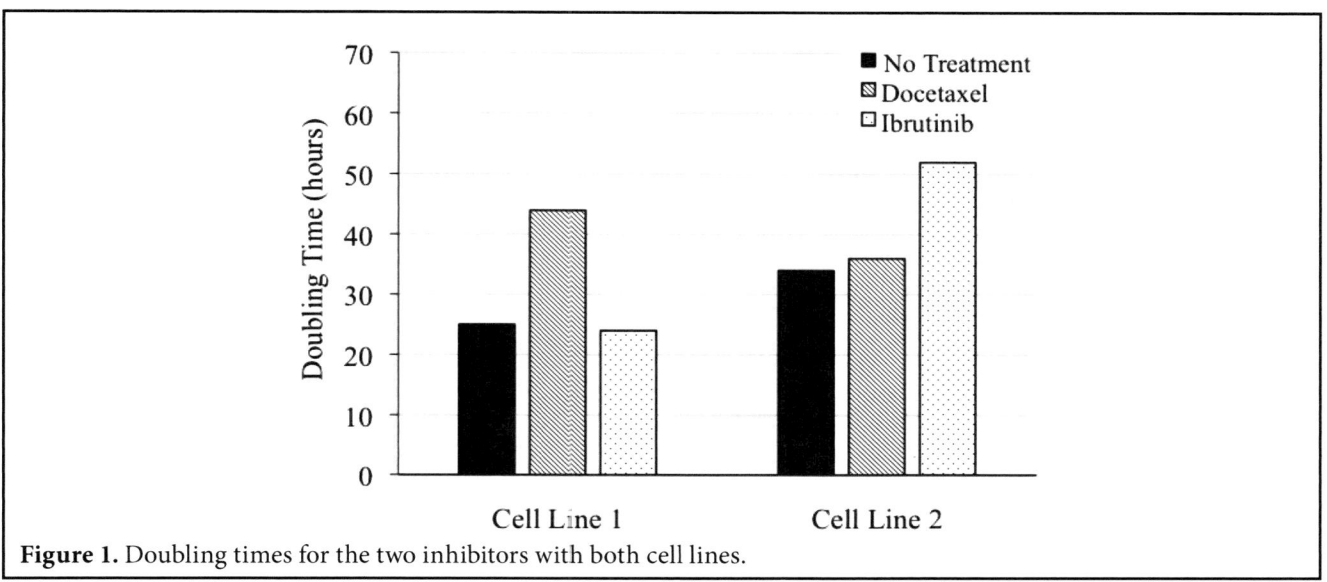

Figure 1. Doubling times for the two inhibitors with both cell lines.

1. Chromosomal crossover, or the exchange of genetic information between homologous chromosomes, occurs in which stage of mitosis?

   Example: *Because the passage does not discuss crossover, our answer must be derived from content knowledge alone. Crossover occurs between homologous chromosomes during prophase I of meiosis. The question stem asks which stage of* mitosis, *so we should look for any answer choices that deal with* meiosis *instead.*

2. Among non-cancerous cells in the human body, which cells are likely to undergo mitosis at the fastest rate?

3. The restriction point, or the point at which a cell is committed to undergoing mitosis, is located in which stage of interphase?

4. If the researcher examines Cell Line 1 in the presence of docetaxel under a microscope, would the majority be in interphase or a mitotic phase?

5. Answer the Question
   - If you have not done so already, try to eliminate at least two answer choices.
   - Identify the concept each answer choice represents and compare to your prediction.
   - Compare the two remaining answer choices.
   - Identify fatal flaws in either answer choice.
   - Eliminate absolute or extreme answer choices (i.e., *only, best, never,* etc.) in favor of more flexible terms (i.e., *sometimes, may, can,* etc.).
   - Ensure that the correct answer is accurate *and* addresses the question.
   - *Never* leave a question blank.

Use the recommended question strategies to find the correct answer to each question.

1. Chromosomal crossover, or the exchange of genetic information between homologous chromosomes, occurs in which stage of mitosis?
   A. Prophase
   B. Metaphase II
   C. Anaphase
   D. None of these

   Example: *Based on our prediction, we are looking for prophase I of meiosis as our answer, so we can easily eliminate answer choices B and C. Answer choice A is also incorrect because crossover occurs during prophase I of* meiosis, *not* mitosis, *which is suggested by the question stem. Although "none of the above" is rarely the correct answer, we know that answer choice D must be correct by elimination.*

2. Among non-cancerous cells in the human body, which cells are likely to undergo mitosis at the fastest rate?
   A. Neurons
   B. Muscle cells
   C. Skin cells
   D. Germ cells

3. The restriction point, or the point at which a cell is committed to undergoing mitosis, is located in which stage of interphase?
   A. G0
   B. S
   C. G1
   D. G2

4. If the researcher examines Cell Line 1 in the presence of docetaxel under a microscope, would the majority be in interphase or a mitotic phase?
   A. Interphase, because docetaxel will prevent the microtubule-organizing center (MTOC) from developing during this stage
   B. A mitotic phase, because docetaxel will prevent formation of the cleavage furrow during cytokinesis
   C. Interphase, because docetaxel will prevent DNA duplication
   D. A mitotic phase, because docetaxel will arrest the cells in mitosis prior to anaphase

Solutions:

1. D

2. C

3. C

4. A

Science Recall Question Strategy

> Science Identification and Recall is tested on discrete questions and requires you to identify and recall information from your content knowledge.
> The same strategies apply as with Science Reasoning except that you will only need to draw on information from your content knowledge base:

1. Translate the Question
2. Research and Predict an Answer
3. Answer the Question

Use the recommended question strategies to find the correct answer to each question.

1. How does cDNA differ from eukaryotic DNA?
    A. It is artificially made in a lab.
    B. It has post-transcriptional modifications, such as a 5' cap.
    C. It lacks exons.
    D. It lacks introns.

2. Where do post-transcriptional modifications of RNA take place?
    A. In the nucleus of the cell
    B. In the cytoplasm of the cell
    C. Mainly in the nucleus, but also in the cytoplasm
    D. Mainly in the cytoplasm, but also in the nucleus

3. Which of the following are necessary post-transcriptional modifications for export of eukaryotic mRNA to the cytoplasm?
   A. Addition of a poly-A tail
   B. Splicing
   C. 3' Guanine cap
   D. A and B

4. If baldness is an X-linked recessive disorder, which of the following could NOT also have been a carrier of the gene or genes resulting in a man's baldness?
   A. The bald male's mother
   B. The bald male's maternal grandmother
   C. The bald male's paternal grandmother
   D. The bald male's maternal grandfather

5. The heart, femur, and bicep most likely arise from which of the following primary germ layers?
   A. Endoderm
   B. Mesoderm
   C. Ectoderm
   D. Morula

Solutions:

1. D
2. A
3. D
4. D
5. B

Practice Cooldown

1. The catabolism of which fuel yields the highest ATP output under aerobic conditions?
   A. Sugars
   B. Fatty acids
   C. Proteins
   D. Vitamins

2. Starch in the digestive system is broken down by which enzyme?
   A. Lysozyme
   B. Amylase
   C. Pepsin
   D. Trypsin

3. Translation can be inhibited by certain antibiotics that affect bacterial ribosomes. Why are these antibiotics not harmful to human cells?
   A. These antibiotics target the 40S ribosomal subunit.
   B. Eukaryotic ribosomes are protected by their own membranes.
   C. These antibiotics target the 50S ribosomal subunit.
   D. These antibiotics bind to tRNA when in the A site.

4. Which of these organisms possess membrane-bound organelles?
   A. Protozoa
   B. Bacteriophages
   C. Archaea
   D. Bacteria

5. A patient's blood is cultured and returns a positive test for peptidoglycan. This patient likely suffers from which type of infection?
   A. A fungal infection
   B. A viral infection
   C. A parasitic infection
   D. A bacterial infection

6. Plasmid exchange between bacteria is also known as:
   A. transformation.
   B. transduction.
   C. transposition.
   D. conjugation.

7. All of the following statements are true of viruses EXCEPT:
   A. they are composed of proteins and nucleic acids.
   B. they often mutate at a high rate.
   C. they contain a number of simple membranous organelles.
   D. they are incapable of replicating without a host cell.

8. A congenital dysfunction in the behavior of chondrocytes would LEAST likely make a patient prone to:
   A. knee pain.
   B. herniated discs.
   C. torn calf muscles.
   D. ankle sprains.

9. A cardiologist takes a biopsy of muscle tissue from the wall of the superior vena cava. Upon analysis of this tissue, what characteristics would he find?
   A. Multinucleate, striated fibers with clearly defined sarcomeres
   B. Uninucleate, non-striated cells with tapered ends
   C. Highly branched, striated fibers that mainly appear to be uninucleate
   D. As a vein, the vena cava does not contain muscle.

10. All of the structures below represent long bones EXCEPT:
    A. the humerus.
    B. the femur.
    C. the mandible.
    D. the tibia.

To Do After Lesson 11

- ❏ Read Chemical Processes Ch. 24–25
- ❏ Complete CP Ch. 24–25 End of Chapter Questions

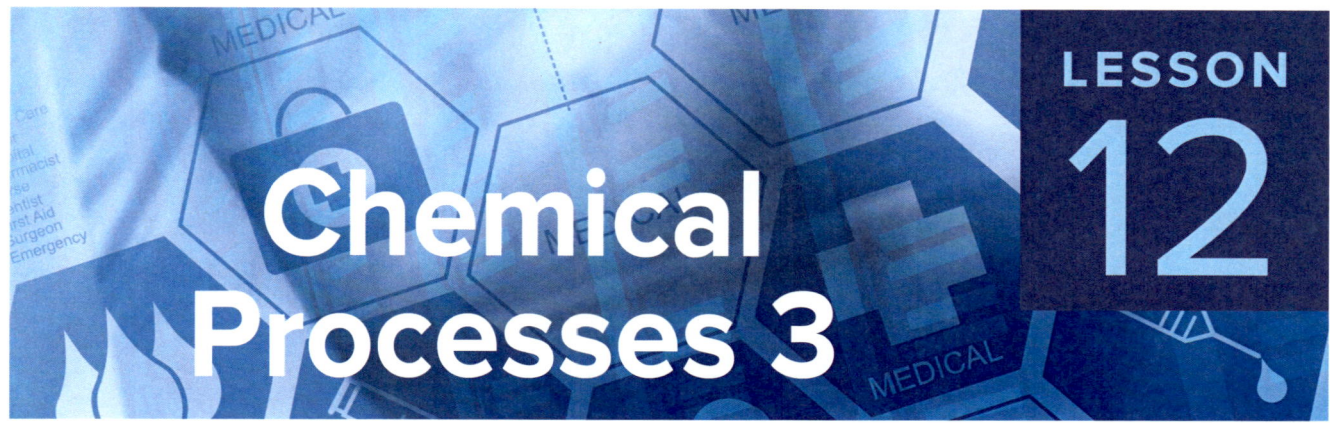

Chemical Processes 3

LESSON 12

To Do Before Lesson 12

- ❑ Read Chemical Processes Ch. 24–25
- ❑ Complete CP Ch. 24–25 End of Chapter Questions

In Lesson 12

- > Science Reasoning Question Strategy
- > Science Recall Question Strategy
- > Practice Cooldown

To Do After Lesson 12

- ❑ Read Quantitative Reasoning Ch. 32
- ❑ Complete QR Ch. 32 End of Chapter Questions

Science Reasoning Question Strategy

> Science Reasoning is tested on questions associated with passages and requires you to apply your content knowledge to new information.

1. Translate the Question

> Simply translate the question into what it is *really* asking.
> - What content topic or equation is the question addressing?
> - What passage information is being tested?
>
> Rephrase "except" or "not" question in a way that makes sense to you.

Re-read the passage below (from Lesson 9) and translate the following questions associated with this passage into what they are really asking.

POLYPEPTIDES

The structure of a polypeptide was determined beginning with the identification of its constituent amino acids. A purified sample of the polypeptide was denatured and then hydrolyzed by a strong acid at 110°C for 24 hours. The individual amino acids released by the treatment were then separated by cation-exchange chromatography. In this technique, amino acids bind with differing affinities to negatively-charged groups attached to resins along the column.

Following treatment with a series of eluting solutions, the separated amino acids in the eluate were heated with ninhydrin—a reagent that forms the blue-purple compound Ruhemann's Purple with most amino acids, amines, and ammonia.

Figure 1. The ninhydrin reaction between ninhydrin and a free amino acid.

The amount of each amino acid present was then determined spectrophotometrically by measuring the amount of blue-purple light absorbed.

The specific position of each amino acid in the polypeptide chain was also determined. Edman reagent (phenylisothiocyanate) was used to label a terminal residue under mildly alkaline conditions, resulting in the formation of a phenylthiocarbamoyl. Under acidic conditions, the terminal amino acid of the polypeptide was cleaved, releasing free polypeptide and phenylthiohydantoin (PTH), an amino acid derivative. Edman reagent was applied repeatedly, shortening the peptide bond obtained following each cycle. The steps of the Edman degradation are shown in Figure 2.

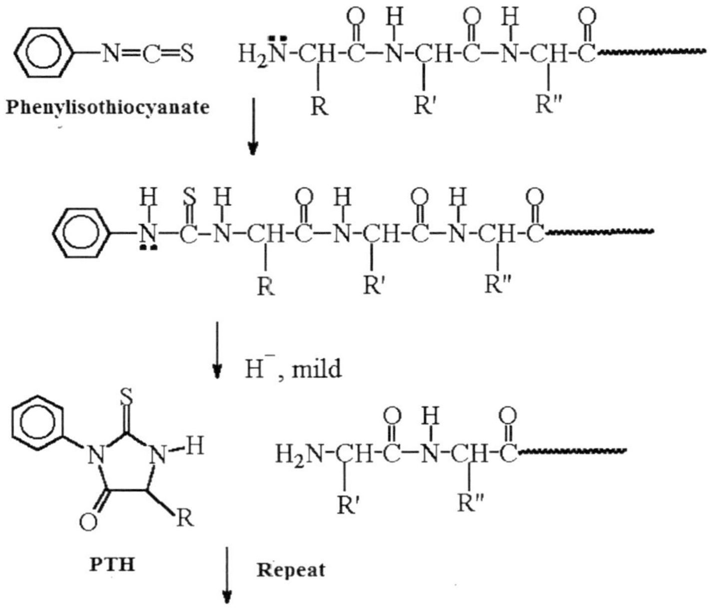

Figure 2. Edman degradation of a polypeptide.

There are limits on the length of polypeptides that can be sequenced by this method. Over time, the yield of PTH-amino acid products decreases relative to the background level of PTH-amino acids. Repetitive yield is a measure of the percent of detectable material remaining after each turn of the cycle. Longer polypeptides can be sequenced from greater initial sample sizes and larger repetitive yields. They may also be cleaved by peptidase enzymes to create shorter polypeptides for sequencing.

5. What is most likely true of the eluent solutions used to recover free amino acids from the ion-exchange column employed?

   Example: *What will disrupt binding of amino acids to the ion-exchange column? This requires content knowledge about ion-exchange chromatography and passage information in Paragraph 1 about amino acids binding negatively-charged residues in cation-exchange columns.*

6. Unfolding of the polypeptide in the presence of the denaturant proceeded via a unimolecular mechanism with rate constant k. What are the units for k?

   _____

   _____

   _____

7. Which of the following reaction types best describes the formation of the bond between phenylisothiocyanate and a polypeptide during the first reaction in Figure 2?

   _____

   _____

   _____

8. The final product in Figure 1 possesses which of the following functional groups?

   _____

   _____

   _____

2. Research and Predict an Answer

- What information do you need to answer this question?
   a. Content knowledge? Passage information? Both?
- Research the idea mentioned in the question stem by locating it in the passage.
- Make a prediction and eliminate answer choices that do not fit.
- Research the remaining answer choices in the passage.

LESSON 12: CHEMICAL PROCESSES 3

Find the location of the idea tested by each question in the passage, if possible, and make a prediction for each. The first question has been completed as an example.

POLYPEPTIDES

The structure of a polypeptide was determined beginning with the identification of its constituent amino acids. A purified sample of the polypeptide was denatured and then hydrolyzed by a strong acid at 110°C for 24 hours. The individual amino acids released by the treatment were then separated by ==cation-exchange chromatography==. In this technique, ==amino acids bind== with differing affinities ==to negatively-charged groups== attached to resins along the column.

Following treatment with a series of eluting solutions, the separated amino acids in the eluate were heated with ninhydrin—a reagent that forms the blue-purple compound Ruhemann's Purple with most amino acids, amines, and ammonia.

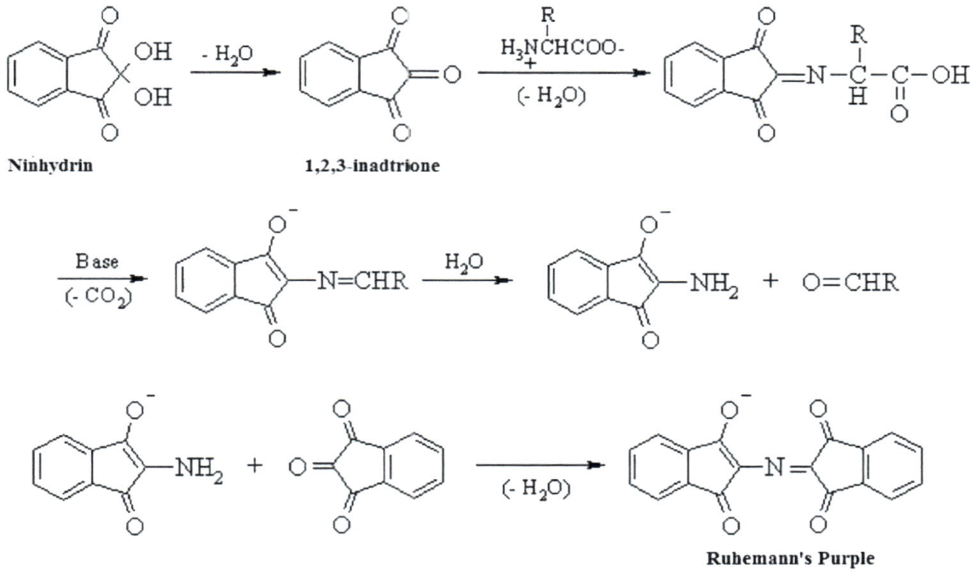

Figure 1. The ninhydrin reaction between ninhydrin and a free amino acid.

The amount of each amino acid present was then determined spectrophotometrically by measuring the amount of blue-purple light absorbed.

The specific position of each amino acid in the polypeptide chain was also determined. Edman reagent (phenylisothiocyanate) was used to label a terminal residue under mildly alkaline conditions, resulting in the formation of a phenylthiocarbamoyl. Under acidic conditions, the terminal amino acid of the polypeptide was cleaved, releasing free polypeptide and phenylthiohydantoin (PTH), an amino acid derivative. Edman reagent was applied repeatedly, shortening the peptide bond obtained following each cycle. The steps of the Edman degradation are shown in Figure 2.

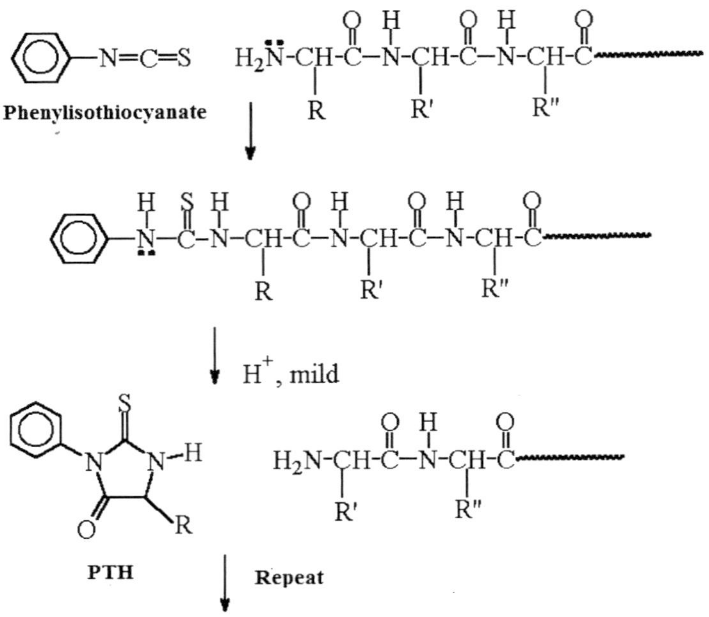

Figure 2. Edman degradation of a polypeptide.

There are limits on the length of polypeptides that can be sequenced by this method. Over time, the yield of PTH-amino acid products decreases relative to the background level of PTH-amino acids. Repetitive yield is a measure of the percent of detectable material remaining after each turn of the cycle. Longer polypeptides can be sequenced from greater initial sample sizes and larger repetitive yields. They may also be cleaved by peptidase enzymes to create shorter polypeptides for sequencing.

1. What is most likely true of the eluent solutions used to recover free amino acids from the ion-exchange column employed?

    Example: *As stated in Paragraph 1, free amino acids are bound to negatively-charged resins in the column. From content knowledge, we know that the amino acids participating in ionic bonding with the column resins must be positively-charged. If we make the charge on the amino acids more neutral, they will dissociate from the column. We can achieve this by raising the pH of the eluent to deprotonate the free amino acids, or by changing the salt concentration of the buffer to compete with and disrupt the ionic interactions on the column.*

2. Unfolding of the polypeptide in the presence of the denaturant proceeded via a unimolecular mechanism with rate constant k. What are the units for k?

3. Which of the following reaction types best describes the formation of the bond between phenylisothiocyanate and a polypeptide during the first reaction in Figure 2?

4. The final product in Figure 1 possesses which of the following functional groups?

3. Answer the Question

> - Try to eliminate at least two answer choices
> - Identify the concept each answer choice represents and compare to your prediction
> - Compare the two remaining answer choices
> - Identify fatal flaws in either answer choice
> - Eliminate absolute or extreme answer choices (i.e., *only, best, never,* etc.) in favor of more flexible terms (i.e., *sometimes, may, can,* etc.)
> - Ensure that the correct answer is accurate *and* addresses the question
> - *Never* leave a question blank

Use the recommended question strategies to find the correct answer to each question.

1. What is most likely true of the eluent solutions used to recover free amino acids from the ion-exchange column employed?
   A. They are hydrophobic.
   B. They possess a characteristic salt concentration.
   C. They must be capable of denaturing disulfide linkages.
   D. They must contain digestive enzymes.

   Example: *We are looking for an answer choice that describes pH or salt changes in eluent. Answer choice B is the best fit! Answer choices C and D are not appropriate because the analyte in question consists of free amino acids, not peptide chains. A hydrophobic eluent (A) could work in thin layer or liquid chromatography with a nonpolar eluent but will not work in ion-exchange chromatography.*

2. Unfolding of the polypeptide in the presence of the denaturant proceeded via a unimolecular mechanism with rate constant k. What are the units for k?
   A. s^{-1}
   B. $M\ s$
   C. $M^{-1}\ s^{-1}$
   D. $M\ s^{-1}$

3. Which of the following reaction types best describes the formation of the bond between phenylisothiocyanate and a polypeptide during the first reaction in Figure 2?
   A. Addition
   B. Dehydration
   C. Neutralization
   D. Elimination

4. The final product in Figure 1 possesses which of the following functional groups?
    A. Amine
    B. Ester
    C. Imine
    D. Amide

Solutions:

1. B

2. A

3. A

4. C

NextStepTESTPREP.com

Science Recall Question Strategy

> Science Identification and Recall is tested on discrete questions and requires you to identify and recall information from your content knowledge, but the same strategies apply:

1. Translate the Question
2. Research and Predict an Answer
3. Answer the Question

Use the recommended question strategies to find the correct answer to each question.

1. What happens to the K_{eq} of a reaction when a catalyst is added?

    A. K_{eq} will decrease.
    B. K_{eq} will increase.
    C. K_{eq} will remain the same.
    D. K_{eq} will increase, and then decrease.

2. The chemical formula of calcium phosphate is:
    A. $CaPO_4$
    B. Ca_3PO_4
    C. $Ca_2(PO_4)_3$
    D. $Ca_3(PO_4)_2$

3. The pK$_a$ of acetic acid (HC$_2$H$_3$O$_2$) is 4.8. What is the pH of a 0.10 M solution of sodium acetate?
   A. 2.9
   B. 7.0
   C. 8.9
   D. 13.0

4. Which of the following compounds has the highest boiling point?
   A. H$_2$O
   B. CH$_4$
   C. NH$_3$
   D. HF

5. What is the percent mass composition of oxygen in hydrogen peroxide (H$_2$O$_2$)?
   A. 5.9%
   B. 11.8%
   C. 47.1%
   D. 94.1%

Solutions:

1. C
2. D
3. C
4. A
5. D

Practice Cooldown

1. Cobalt-60 has a half-life of 5.2 years. How much cobalt-60 will remain after 26 years if you begin with 32 grams of the isotope?
   A. 0 grams
   B. 1 gram
   C. 2 grams
   D. 4 grams

2. If Cl^{37} were to emit a gamma particle, the nucleus of which element would be left?
   A. Potassium
   B. Sulfur
   C. Argon
   D. Chlorine

3. A certain element decays once, leaving behind a positron and Na^{24}. The initial element must have been:
   A. Al^{28}
   B. Ne^{24}
   C. Mg^{24}
   D. Na^{24}

4. A polycyclic species is shown below. How many stereocenters are present in this molecule?

   A. 5
   B. 7
   C. 9
   D. 10

5. The total number of possible structural isomers of pentane is:
   A. two.
   B. three.
   C. four.
   D. five.

6. This conformer shown below can be described as:

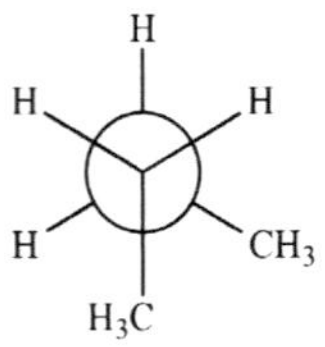

   A. anti.
   B. eclipsed.
   C. totally eclipsed.
   D. gauche.

7. The diagram below shows two straight-chain sugars in the form of Fischer projections. These structures can be described as:

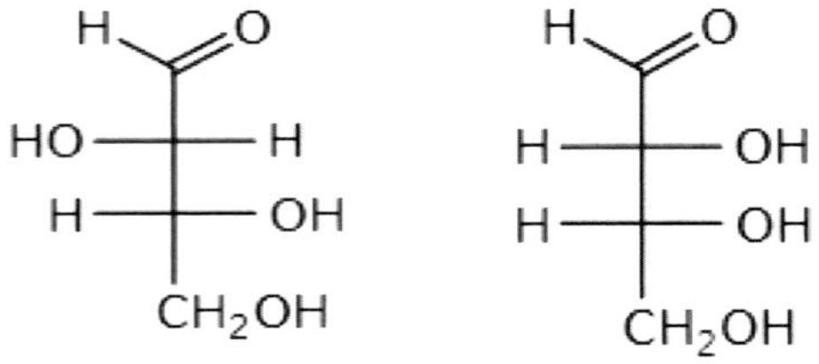

   Images adapted from Christopher King under CC BY-SA 3.0

   A. enantiomers.
   B. meso compounds.
   C. diastereomers.
   D. identical molecules.

8. The concentration of a dilute solution of D-lactose was determined to be 0.3 g/mL. If the specific rotation of D-lactose is +52.3° and the path length is 1 dm, what must be the observed optical rotation when this mixture is exposed to plane-polarized light? Note $[\alpha] = \frac{\alpha}{cl}$.
   A. -27.6°
   B. -17.4°
   C. +15.7°
   D. +174.3°

9. What is the IUPAC name for this molecule?

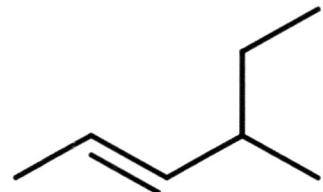

   A. *Trans*-3-methyl-4-hexene
   B. *Trans*-4-ethyl-2-pentene
   C. *Trans*-4-methyl-2-hexene
   D. *Trans*-4-methyl-3-hexene

10. A fatty acid that contains three carbon-carbon double bonds, as well as one carbon-oxygen double bond, is termed a:
    A. polyunsaturated fatty acid.
    B. saturated fatty acid.
    C. monounsaturated fatty acid.
    D. tetraunsaturated fatty acid.

To Do After Lesson 12

- ❏ Read Quantitative Reasoning Ch. 32
- ❏ Complete QR Ch. 32 End of Chapter Questions

This page left intentionally blank.

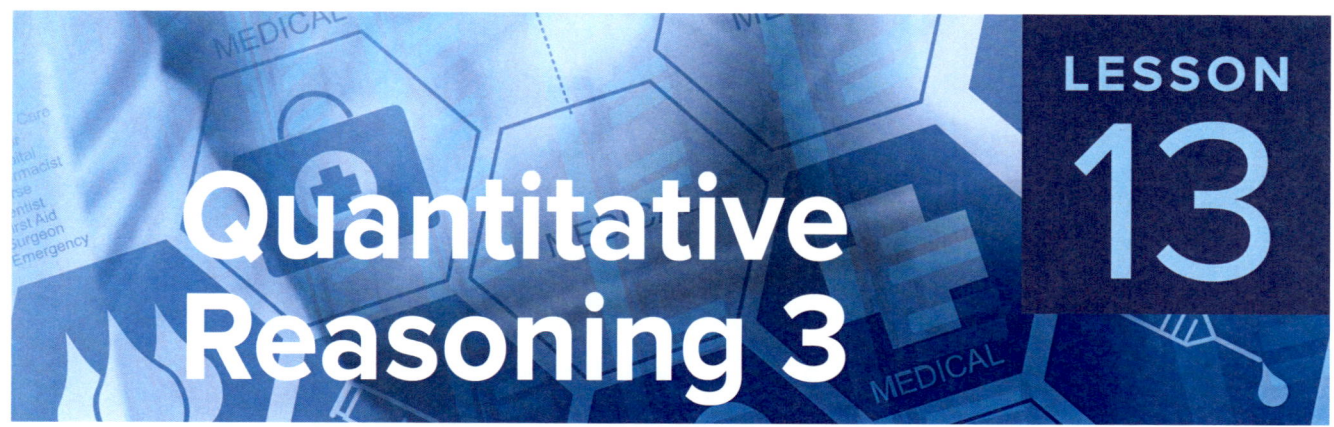

Lesson 13: Quantitative Reasoning 3

To Do Before Lesson 13

- ❏ Read Quantitative Reasoning Ch. 32
- ❏ Complete QR Ch. 32 End of Chapter Questions

In Lesson 13

- > Strategic Practice
- > SWOT Analysis
- > Practice Cooldown

To Do After Lesson 13

- ❏ Complete Quantitative Reasoning Section Review
- ❏ Perform SWOT analysis on QR Section Review
- ❏ Read Biological Processes Ch. 12–14
- ❏ Complete BP Ch. 12–14 End of Chapter Questions

Strategic Practice

> You can *always* make improvements on either your _____ or _____.
> The three stages of practice:

1. Learn
2. Repeat
3. Optimize

Label which stage of practice you think you are in for each of the following problems.

Problem	Practice Stage
1. What is $113.4 \div \sqrt{196}$?	_____
2. Simplify $\log_4 2 - 3\log_4 x$.	_____
3. Solve $(8x+3)(x-1) = 4x^2$.	_____
4. A bag of marbles contains 10 red marbles, 8 blue marbles, and 13 green marbles. If one marble is drawn at random, what is the probability that the marble is green?	_____
5. Evaluate $g(f(-1))$ if $f(x) = \frac{x}{2} + 1$ and $g(x) = x^2 - 4x - 2$.	_____
6. Find the inverse function of $f(x) = 6x^2 - 1$.	_____
7. Find $\lim_{x \to \infty} \frac{2}{x+1}$.	_____
8. Find the derivative of $\frac{5x^9}{3}$.	_____

1. Learn

> Use guided problems in your PCAT book to practice questions to learn how to solve math problems correctly.
> You have "learned" a content area when you can solve several similar problems correctly without guidance.
> Record the methods that have helped you solve problems in your LLJ as if you were teaching another student how to ace the Quantitative Reasoning section.

LESSON 13: QUANTITATIVE REASONING 3

Learn to solve difficult math problems with the following examples.

Find $\lim_{x \to \infty} \frac{2}{x+1}$.

Find the derivative of $\frac{5x^9}{3}$.

Find the inverse function of $f(x)=6x^2-1$.

2. Repeat

> Practice through repetition until you have mastered that content area.
> You have achieved mastery when you can teach this material to someone else.
> Record your strategic insight in your LLJ.

Practice difficult math problems through repetition with the following examples.

Given $f(x)=\frac{x}{2}+1$, $g(x)=x^2-4x-2$, and $h(x)=\frac{1}{x}$, evaluate:

a) $g(f(-1))$

b) $(f \circ g \circ h)(4)$

c) $(f(g)-g)(-6)$

A bag of marbles contains 10 red marbles, 8 blue marbles, and 14 green marbles. What is the probability that:

a) one marble drawn at random is blue?

b) a blue marble AND THEN a green marble are drawn at random, without replacement?

c) a blue marble OR a green marble is drawn at random from one draw?

LESSON 13: QUANTITATIVE REASONING 3

3. Optimize

> Perfect your technique by finding and utilizing the most efficient strategies for problem-solving.

Optimize your strategy for solving difficult math problems with the following examples.

Solve $(4x - 3)(x - 1) = 3x^2 + x$.

Lesson Learned: _____
_____

Simplify $\log_4 2 - 3\log_4 x$.

Lesson Learned: _____
_____

What is $143\sqrt{6} \div \sqrt{196}$?

Lesson Learned: _____
_____

SWOT Analysis

> **Strengths** are internal factors that advantage you
> **Weaknesses** are internal factors that disadvantage you
> **Opportunities** are external factors that can advantage you
> **Threats** are external factors that can disadvantage you

Strengths
- Content areas or PCAT skills that you have mastered

Weaknesses
- Content areas or PCAT skills that need improvement

Opportunities
- Resources to reinforce strengths and strategies to address weaknesses

Threats
- Potential distractions or factors that could impede progress

Test Day Success

Examine the sample SWOT analysis below. Circle the items that would belong in your personal SWOT analysis.

Sample SWOT Analysis

Strengths
- Body systems
- Essay writing
- Basic math and algebra
- Conceptual chemistry problems
- Science recall

Weaknesses
- Chemistry equations
- Calculus
- Solving math problems efficiently
- Critical Reading timing
- Science passage reasoning

Opportunities
- Content Review videos
- Study Plan generator
- End of Chapter questions
- Lessons Learned Journal
- Flashcards

Threats
- Concurrent class schedule
- Fitting in all my resources
- Timing on Quantitative Section
- Test Day anxiety
- Time left until Test Day

Complete the Quantitative Reasoning Section Review and perform a thorough SWOT analysis. Identify at least 5 discrete strengths, weaknesses, opportunities, and threats.

Practice Cooldown

1. What are the domain and range of the function $f(x) = \frac{4}{x-2}$?
   A. Domain: $\{x \in R \mid x \neq 0\}$; range: $\{y \in R \mid y \neq 2\}$
   B. Domain: $\{x \in R \mid x \neq 2\}$; range: $\{y \in R \mid y \neq 0\}$
   C. Domain: $\{y \in R \mid y \neq 0\}$; range: $\{x \in R \mid x \neq 2\}$
   D. Domain: $\{y \in R \mid y \neq 2\}$; range: $\{x \in R \mid x \neq 0\}$

2. Which of the following equations describes the circle graphed below?

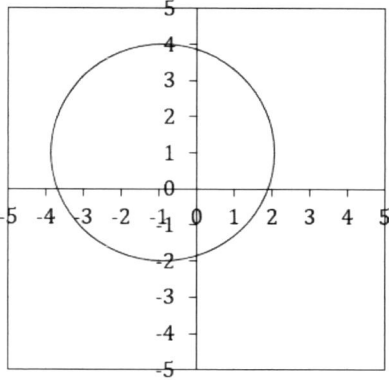

   A. $x^2 + 2x + y^2 - 2y = 7$
   B. $x^2 - 2x + y^2 + 2y = 7$
   C. $X^2 + 2x + y^2 + 2y = 7$
   D. $x^2 - 2x + y^2 - 2y = 7$

3. Find $\frac{d}{dx}\left(\frac{8x^3}{1-x}\right)$.
   A. $\frac{24x^2 - 32x^3}{x^2 - 2x + 1}$
   B. $-24x^2$
   C. $-24x^2 + 1$
   D. $24x^2 - 32x^3$

4. Find $\frac{dy}{dx}(y = 3x^3 + xy^3)$.
   A. $\frac{9x^2}{1 - 3xy^2 + y^3}$
   B. $\frac{9x^2 + y^3}{1 - 3xy^2}$
   C. $9x^2 + 3y^2$
   D. $\frac{9x^2}{1 - 3y^2}$

5. Find $\int \frac{10x^4+3x^{-1/2}}{5} dx$.

   A. $8x^3 + \frac{6}{5x^2} + C$
   B. $\frac{2x^3}{3} + \frac{6x}{5} + C$
   C. $\frac{2}{5}x^5 + \frac{6}{5x} + C$
   D. $\frac{2x^5}{5} + \frac{6}{5}\sqrt{x} + C$

To Do After Lesson 13

- ❑ Complete Quantitative Reasoning Section Review
- ❑ Perform SWOT analysis on QR Section Review
- ❑ Read Biological Processes Ch. 12–14
- ❑ Complete BP Ch. 12–14 End of Chapter Questions

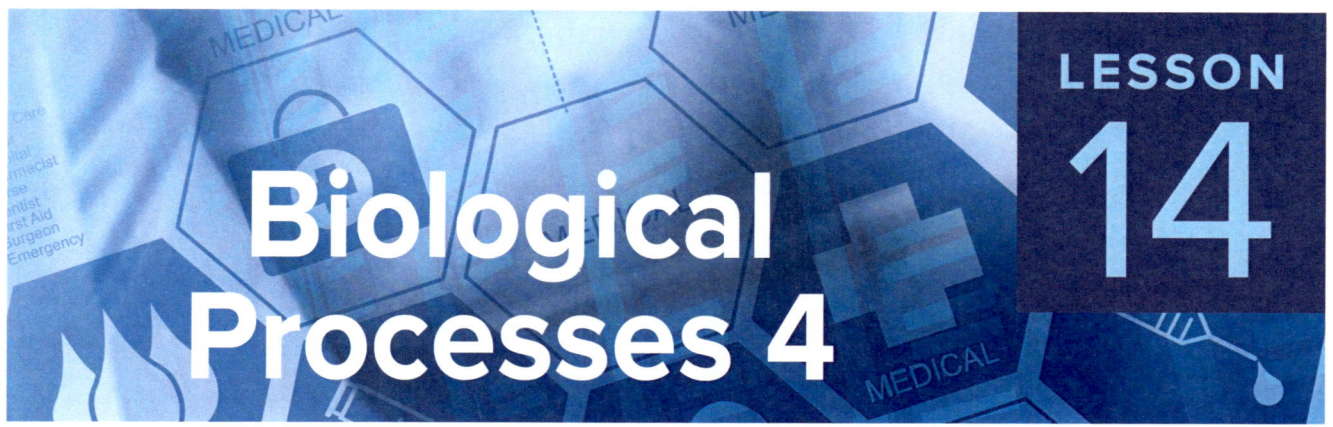

Biological Processes 4

LESSON 14

To Do Before Lesson 14

- ❑ Complete Quantitative Reasoning Section Review
- ❑ Perform SWOT analysis on QR Section Review
- ❑ Read Biological Processes Ch. 12–14
- ❑ Complete BP Ch. 12–14 End of Chapter Questions

In Lesson 14

- > Practice Types
- > Science Foundation
- > Practice Cooldown

To Do After Lesson 14

- ❑ Read Chemical Processes Ch. 26–27
- ❑ Complete CP Ch. 26–27 End of Chapter Questions

NextStepTESTPREP.com

Practice Types

> Your practice should target specific skills you would like to improve, including:
 1. Science Recall (content knowledge, discrete questions)
 2. Science Reasoning (critical thinking, passage-based)
 3. Timing and Endurance
 4. Computer-Based Skills (calculator, periodic table, review screen, typing)

Which strategies and resources will help you improve your *Science Recall*?

Which strategies and resources will help you improve your *Science Reasoning*?

Which strategies and resources will help you improve your *Timing and Endurance*?

LESSON 14: BIOLOGICAL PROCESSES 4

Which strategies and resources will help you improve your Computer-Based Skills?

NextStepTESTPREP.com

Science Foundation

> There are three basic ingredients for building a strong science foundation:
  1. Content Review
  2. Practice
  3. Review
> Utilize your various resources to integrate each method into your study routine
> The more active your practice, the better your retention of the material

Draw and label the organs of the musculoskeletal system on the diagram below: **skull, mandible, maxilla, vertebral column, sacrum, coccyx, rib cage, humerus, ulna, radius, femur, patella, tibia, fibula.**

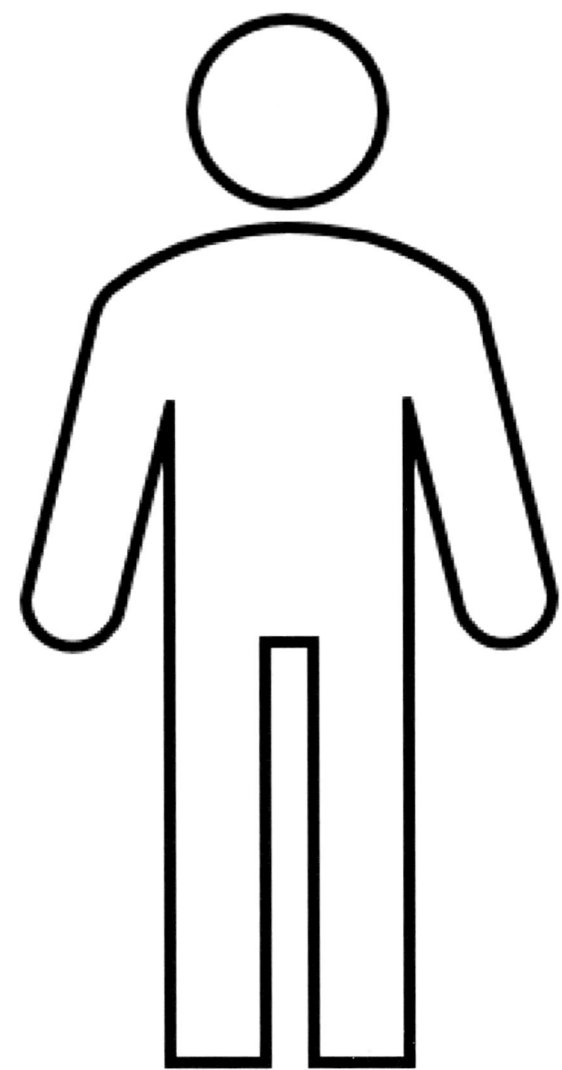

Label the following anatomical positions below: anterior, ventral, posterior, dorsal, cranial, caudal, proximal, distal.

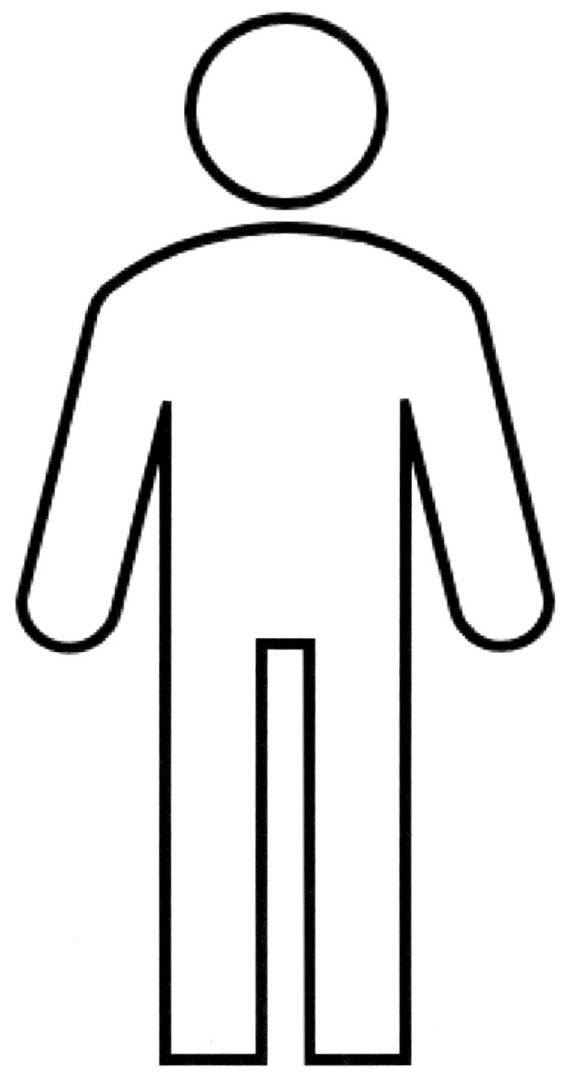

Add notes defining each key term from Chapter 11 on the musculoskeletal system.

cartilage: _____
_____
_____

chondrocytes: _____
_____

collagen: _____

osteocytes: _____

hematopoiesis: _____

adipocytes: _____

acetylcholinesterase: _____

Compare and contrast each pair of key terms from Chapter 11.

ligaments v. tendons: _____

axial v. appendicular skeleton: _____

LESSON 14: BIOLOGICAL PROCESSES 4

exo- v. endoskeleton: _____

_____

_____

diaphysis v. epiphysis: _____

_____

_____

compact v. spongy bone: _____

_____

_____

intramembranous v. endochondral ossification: _____

_____

_____

osteoblasts v. osteoclasts: _____

_____

_____

parathyroid hormone v. calcitonin: _____

_____

_____

red v. yellow marrow: _____

_____

_____

synovial v. cartilaginous v. fibrous joints: _____

summation v. tetanus: _____

Label each structural component on the myocyte shown below with the terms: cisternae, sarcolemma, sarcoplasmic reticulum, triad, T-tubule.

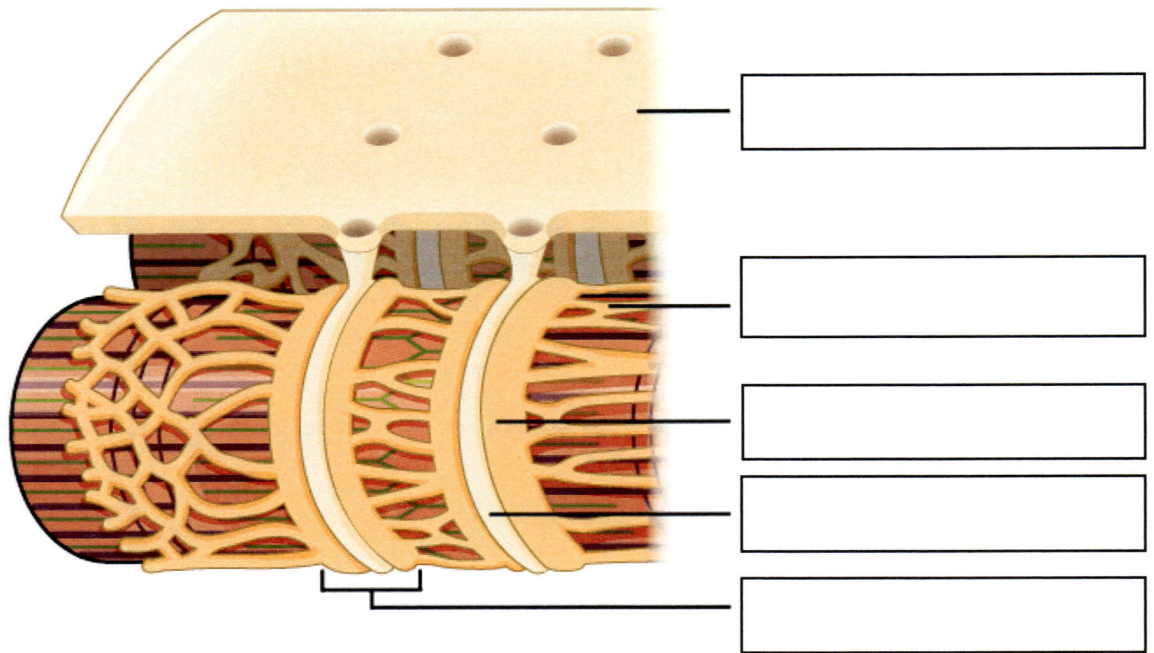

Match each characteristic with the muscle type(s) it represents. Note that there may be more than one matching muscle type.

Smooth Muscle

Cardiac Muscle

Skeletal Muscle

Gap junctions

Involuntary

White fibers

Somatic nervous system

Non-striated

Uninucleate

Voluntary

Intercalated discs

Autonomic nervous system

Red fibers

Pacemaker cells

Peristalsis

Multinucleate

Striated

Label each component of the sarcomere with the following terms and identify how each changes during contraction: actin, myosin, A band, H zone, I band, M line, Z line.

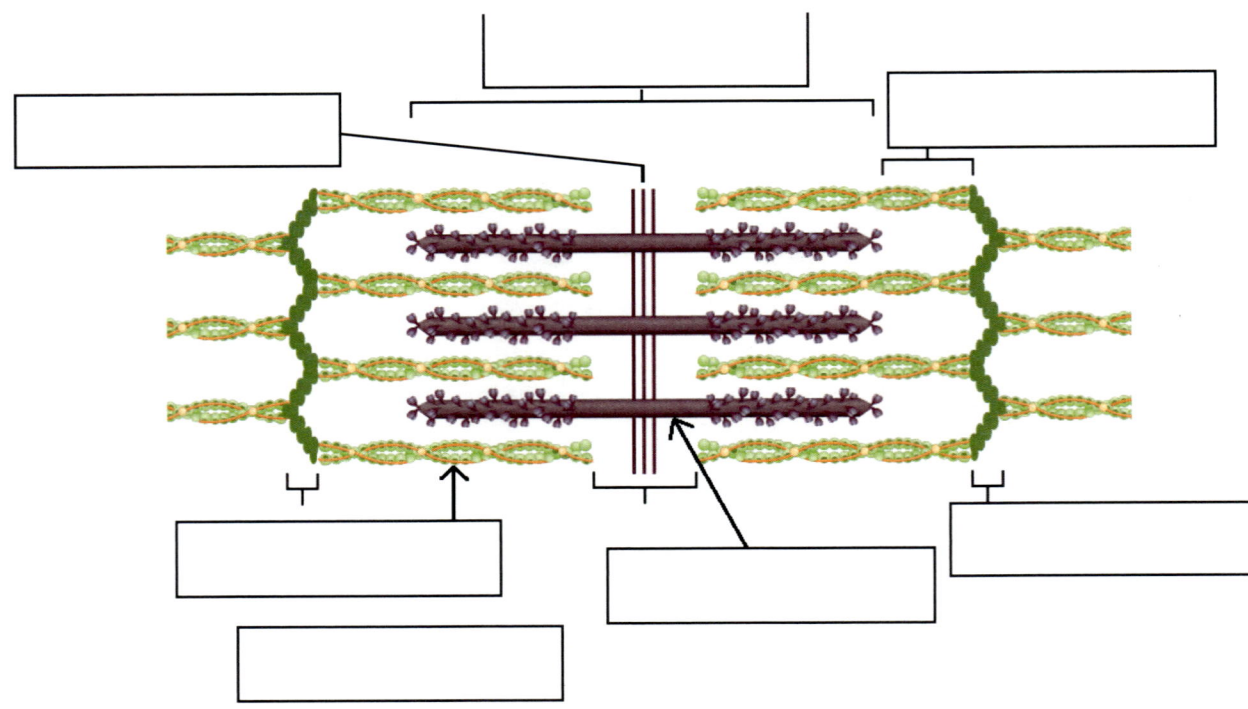

actin:

myosin:

A band:

H zone:

I band:

M line:

Z line:

Sketch the steps of the cross-bridge cycle. The first step has been provided.

Generate 5 questions that you still have about Chapter 11 concepts, and research and document the answers to your questions below.

Question: _____
_____

Answer: _____
_____

Question: _____
_____

Answer: _____
_____

Question: _____
_____

Answer: _____
_____

Question: _____
_____

Answer: _____
_____

Question: _____
_____

Answer: _____
_____

Complete the table below with the divisions of the nervous system from Chapter 12.

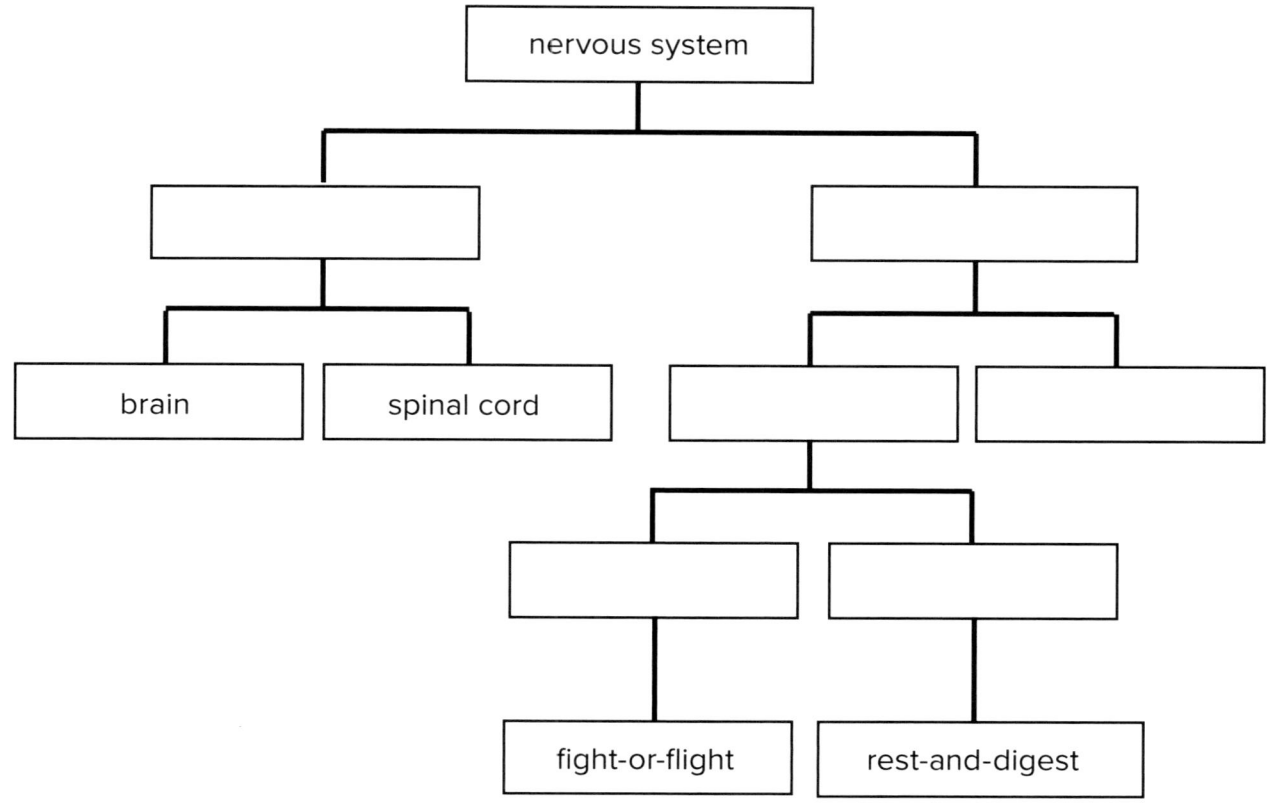

Label the chambers of the heart and draw the direction of blood flow from Chapter 13: aorta, aortic valve, left atrium, left ventricle, mitral valve, pulmonary artery, pulmonary valve, right atrium, right ventricle, tricuspid valve.

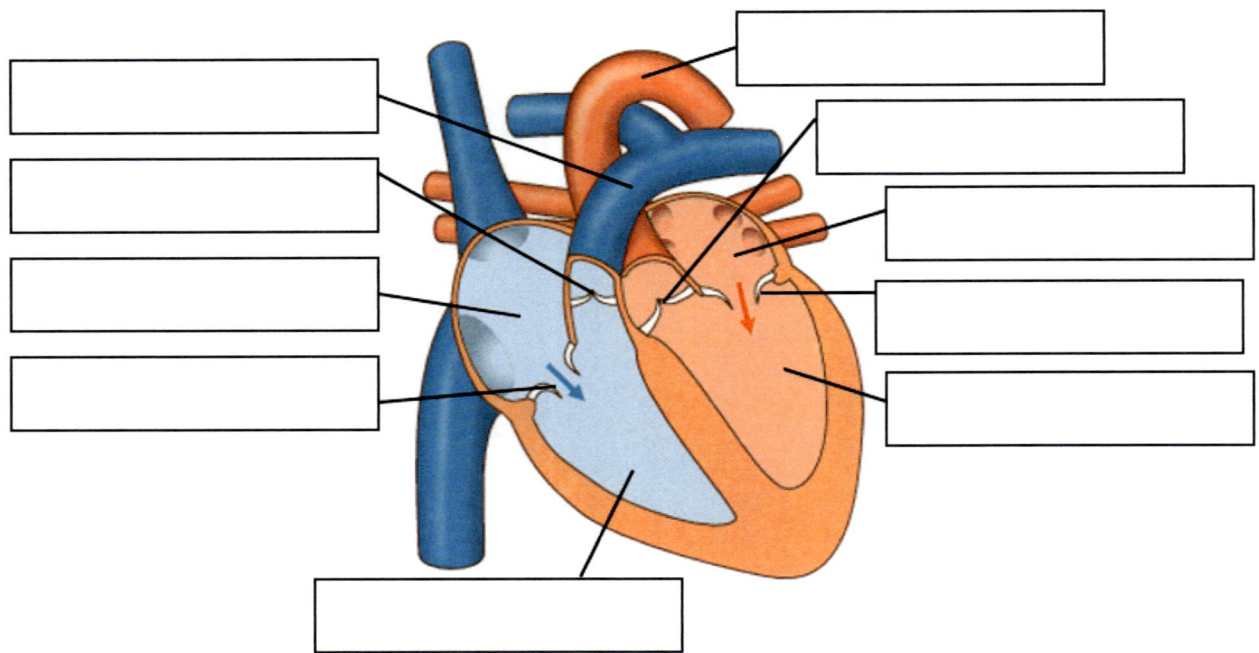

Practice Cooldown

1. A hippocampal neuron with which of the following membrane potentials would most likely be considered to be hyperpolarized?
   A. +40 mV
   B. 0 mV
   C. -70 mV
   D. -85 mV

2. Which of the following hypothetical axons would likely propagate action potentials at the highest conducting velocity?
   A. An unmyelinated axon with a diameter of 1.0 micron
   B. A myelinated axon with a diameter of 1.0 micron
   C. An unmyelinated axon with a diameter of 4.0 microns
   D. A myelinated axon with a diameter of 4.0 microns

3. Locked-in syndrome is a condition in which the sufferer is otherwise healthy and aware of his surroundings, but cannot move or communicate due to paralysis of voluntary muscles. This results from a blockage of:
   A. afferent autonomic pathways.
   B. afferent somatic pathways.
   C. efferent autonomic pathways.
   D. efferent somatic pathways.

4. A patient suffers from persistent indigestion and tachycardia, and various diagnostic tests reveal that his condition is neurological in origin. His symptoms are likely caused by diminished activation of:
   A. the sympathetic nervous system.
   B. the parasympathetic nervous system.
   C. the limbic system.
   D. the somatic nervous system.

5. The partial pressure of CO_2 is highest in part of the circulatory system?
   A. Aorta
   B. Pulmonary artery
   C. Pulmonary veins
   D. The partial pressure of CO_2 is roughly equal in all regions of the heart; it is the O_2 partial pressure that differs.

6. A typical human red blood cell remains in circulation for approximately four months before being cleared by the spleen. Which characteristic of erythrocytes contributes to their short period of viability?
   A. Erythrocytes have no mitochondria and have very low metabolic capabilities, reducing their capacity for cellular repair.
   B. Since mature erythrocytes are anucleate and lack ribosomes, they do not contain any functioning enzymes.
   C. Erythrocytes are exposed to high concentrations of oxygen free radicals, placing them at high risk for becoming cancerous.
   D. Erythrocytes are frequent targets of viral infection due to their limited ability to produce antiviral peptides.

7. Which of the following is LEAST likely to reduce the oxygen-carrying capacity of human blood?
   A. Complete removal of the stomach
   B. Ablation of red bone marrow
   C. Dietary iron deficiency
   D. Intravenous erythropoietin supplementation

8. Hemoglobin can bind a total of four oxygen molecules. Which of these molecules binds with most ease?
   A. The first oxygen
   B. The second oxygen
   C. The third oxygen
   D. The fourth oxygen

9. During pregnancy, the fetus acquires oxygen not through active breathing, but via gas exchange with its mother. In order for this to happen, what must the dissociation curve for fetal hemoglobin look like?
   A. The curve is shifted to the right because fetal hemoglobin has a higher affinity for oxygen than does adult hemoglobin.
   B. The curve is shifted to the left to allow for the diffusion of oxygen through the placenta.
   C. The curve is shifted to the right because maternal hemoglobin diffuses into the fetal bloodstream directly.
   D. The curve is shifted to the left because fetal hemoglobin is composed of different subunits with increased oxygen affinity.

10. How does hyperventilation affect the pH of the blood?
    A. Increased breathing rate results in a lower pH.
    B. Decreased breathing rate results in a higher pH.
    C. Increased breathing rate results in a higher pH.
    D. Decreased breathing rate results in an unchanged pH.

To Do After Lesson 14

❑ Read Chemical Processes Ch. 26–27
❑ Complete CP Ch. 26–27 End of Chapter Questions

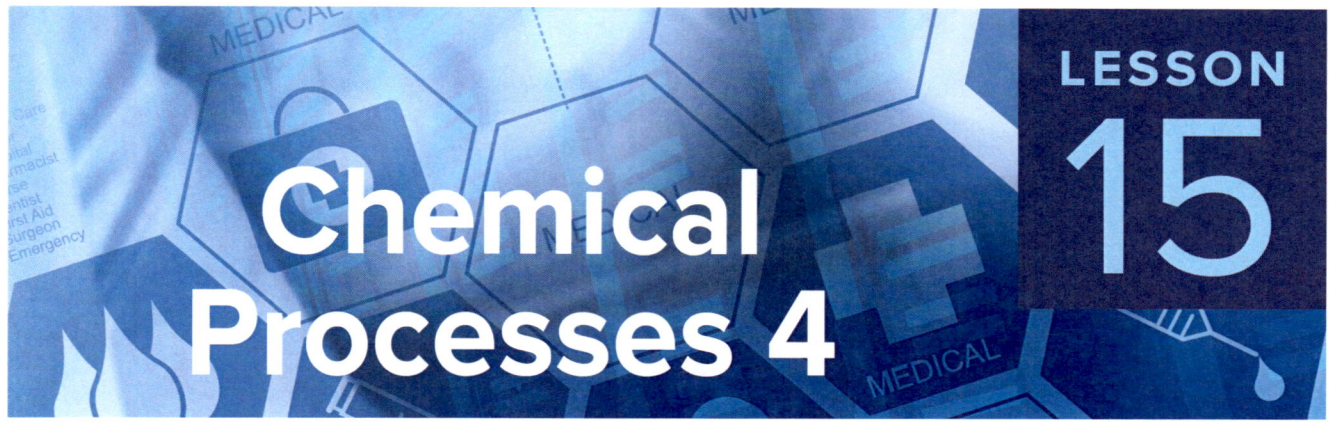

Chemical Processes 4

To Do Before Lesson 15
- ❏ Read Chemical Processes Ch. 26–27
- ❏ Complete CP Ch. 26–27 End of Chapter Questions

In Lesson 15
> Science Foundation
> Practice Cooldown

To Do After Lesson 15
- ❏ Complete Chemical Processes Section Review
- ❏ Perform SWOT Analysis on CP Section Review
- ❏ Complete Full-Length 2
- ❏ Review Full-Length 2

Science Foundation

> The Chemical Processes section is especially well-suited for certain approaches
1. Flashcards
2. Formula Sheets or Tables
3. Visuals
4. Units Practice
> Take your notes in a form that will allow you to study them later, such as flashcards or questions

Draw the following organic molecules.

4-methylpentan-2-one

butanoic acid

3,3-dimethyl-1-butyne

tert-butylcyclohexane

2-propen-1-ol

Name the following organic molecules according to IUPAC nomenclature.

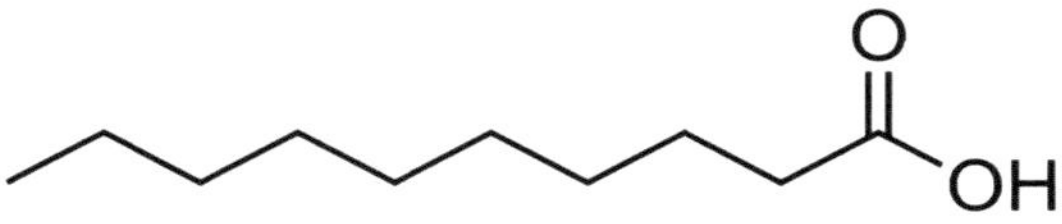

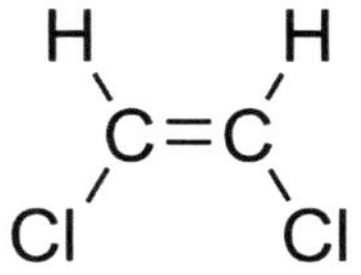

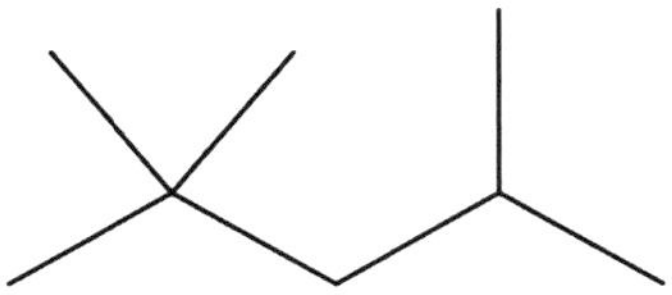

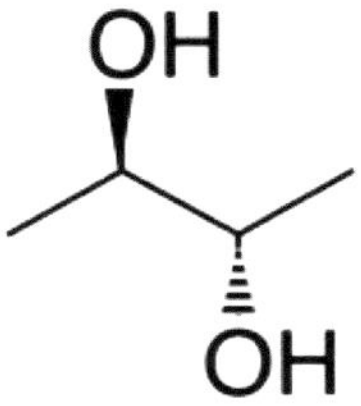

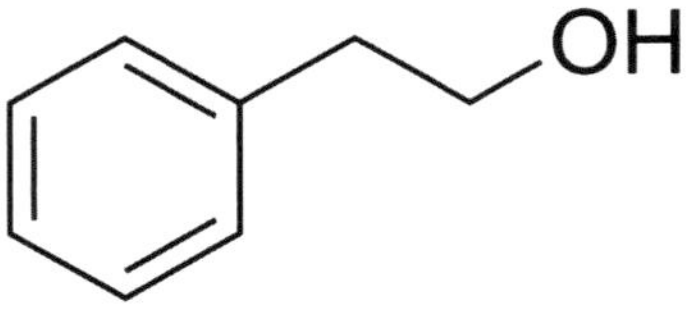

1. nonanoic acid

2. (E)-1,2-dichloroethene

3. 2,2,4-trimethylpentane

4. (2R,3R)-butane-2,3-diol

5. 2-phenylethan-1-ol

Complete the table below with the structures and boiling points (high, medium, low) of the following organic compounds.

NAME	STRUCTURE	MELTING/BOILING POINT
Alkane		
Alkene		
Alkyne		
Alcohol		
Aldehyde		
Ketone		

Carboxylic acid		
Amide		
Ester		
Anhydride		
Amine		

Draw a pair of examples for each of the following.

Structural isomers

Cis-trans isomers

E-Z isomers

Enantiomers

Diastereomers

Meso Compounds

Conformational Isomers

Complete the table below with the properties of S_N1, S_N2, E1, and E2 reactions.

	S_N1	S_N2	E1	E2
Steps				
Rate law				
Substrate Preference (CH3, 1°, 2°, 3°)				
Nucleophile Strength				
Solvent (protic/aprotic)				
Stereochemistry				

NextStepTESTPREP.com

Draw the general schematic for each of the following organic reactions. The first example has been provided.

Reduction

    Aldehyde

    Ketone

    Carboxylic Acid

    Ester

    Alkene

    Alkyne

Lesson Learned:

Oxidation

Primary Alcohol (Weak)

Secondary Alcohol (Weak)

Primary Alcohol (Strong)

Secondary Alcohol (Strong)

Alkene

Lesson Learned:

Water Reactions
    Alkene Hydration

    Alcohol Dehydration

    Ester Hydrolysis

Lesson Learned:

Answer the following questions about the spectrums below.

Spectrum 1

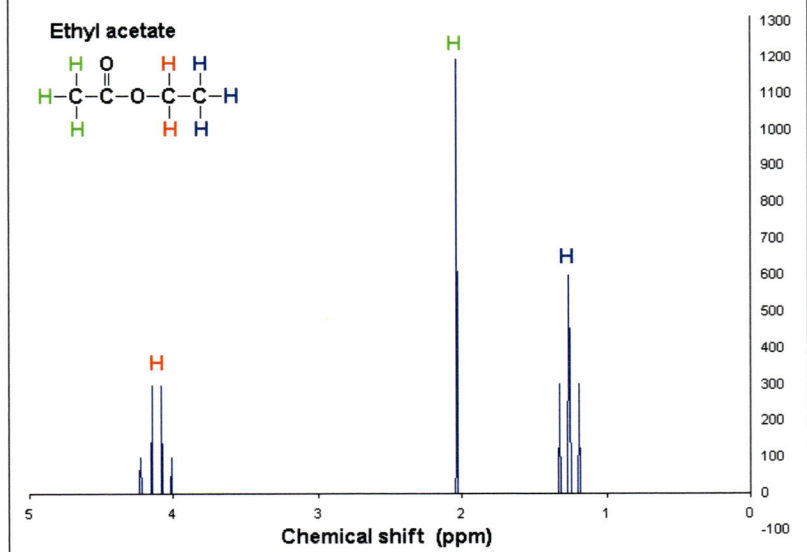

What type of spectroscopy produced Spectrum 1?

_____

What information does this type of spectroscopy collect about organic molecules?

_____

_____

Identify any significant features and mark them on Spectrum 1.

Spectrum 2

What type of spectroscopy produced Spectrum 2?

_____

What information does this type of spectroscopy collect about organic molecules?

_____

_____

Identify any significant features and mark them on Spectrum 2.

Spectrum 3

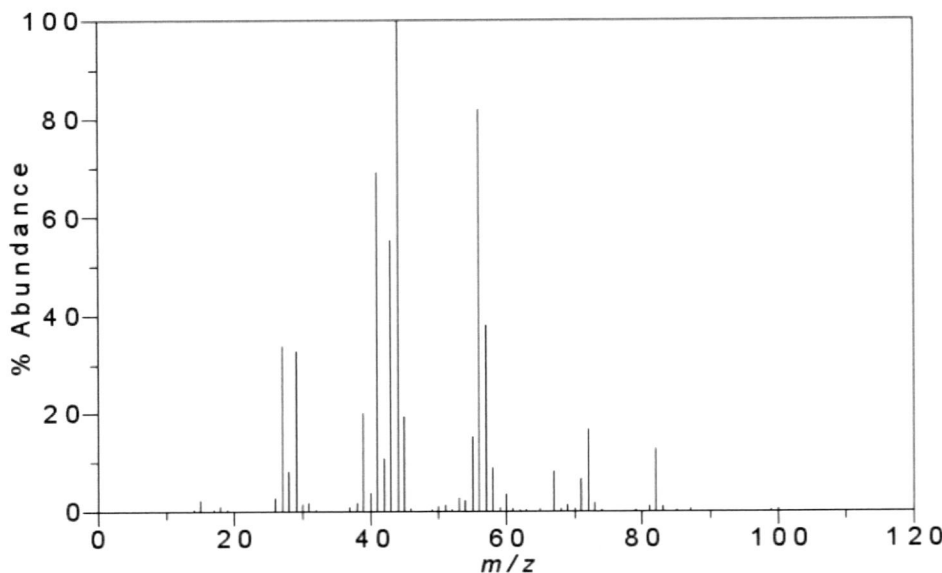

What type of spectroscopy produced Spectrum 3?

_____

What information does this type of spectroscopy collect about organic molecules?

_____

_____

Identify any significant features and mark them on Spectrum 3.

Practice Cooldown

1. A pharmaceutical research team reacts a solution containing an unknown alcohol with $K_2Cr_2O_7$. When this reaction proceeds as desired, Cr^{6+} is reduced to Cr^{3+}, which is indicated by a color change from orange to green. If the solution exhibited no color change, then the unknown alcohol must be:
   A. primary.
   B. tertiary.
   C. primary or tertiary.
   D. secondary or tertiary.

2. A student is searching for the most acidic alcohol to facilitate a certain synthetic procedure. Of the molecules below, which is best suited for his purposes?

   A.

   B.

   C.

   D.

3. How could one best increase the rate of reaction of 1-bromopropane with sodium cyanide?
   A. By doubling the concentration of 1-bromopropane
   B. By doubling the concentration of sodium cyanide
   C. By acidifying the reaction medium
   D. Both choices A and B would increase the reaction rate.

4. Unlike S_N1 reactions, which require at least two steps, S_N2 reactions can proceed through a single transition state. This high-energy species is best described as:
   A. pentavalent, because the nucleophile approaches from the side opposite the leaving group.
   B. pentavalent, because the nucleophile approaches from the same side as the leaving group.
   C. tetrahedral, because the nucleophile approaches the vacant orbital from the same side as the leaving group.
   D. tetrahedral, because the nucleophile can approach the vacant orbital from either side of the species being attacked.

5. Place the following compounds in order of increasing boiling point: water, ethanol, methanol, and acetone.
   A. Water, ethanol, acetone, methanol
   B. Acetone, methanol, ethanol, water
   C. Ethanol, methanol, acetone, water
   D. Water, ethanol, methanol, acetone

6. What product is generated when 2-hexanol successfully reacts with chromium(III) oxide?
   A. Hexanoic acid
   B. 2-Hexanone
   C. Hexane
   D. 1,2-Hexanediol

7. SDS-PAGE is performed on Proteins 1, 2, and 3 using β-mercaptoethanol. From the results below, all of the following can be concluded EXCEPT:

   1 2 3

   A. Protein 2 contains the subunit with the smallest mass in kilodaltons.
   B. Protein 1 contains the subunit with the greatest mass in kilodaltons.
   C. Proteins 1 and 2 might have quaternary structure in their native forms.
   D. Protein 2 has a mass smaller than Protein 3.

8. The enzyme that catalyzes the conversion of glucose into glucose-6-phosphate during glycolysis is most likely which type of enzyme?
   A. Kinase
   B. Phosphatase
   C. Oxidoreductase
   D. None of the above

9. Consider the figure below. What value represents the K_m of this reaction?

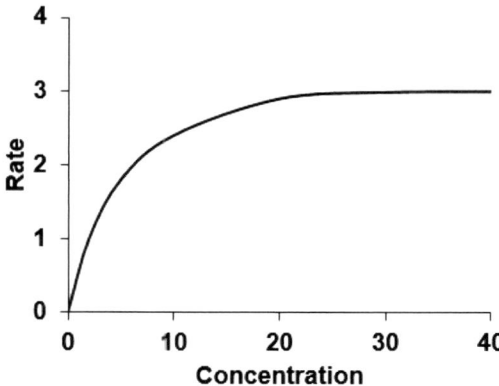

   A. 2
   B. 10
   C. 14
   D. 22

10. Part of a certain amino acid sequence reads KRAKRRH. Where in a protein would this segment most likely be found?
    A. On the surface, because it is mainly hydrophobic
    B. On the surface, because it is mainly hydrophilic
    C. On the interior, because it is mainly hydrophobic
    D. On the interior, because it is mainly hydrophilic

To Do After Lesson 15

- ❏ Complete Chemical Processes Section Review
- ❏ Perform SWOT Analysis on CP Section Review
- ❏ Complete Full-Length 2
- ❏ Review Full-Length 2

This page left intentionally blank.

Quantitative Reasoning 4

LESSON 16

To Do Before Lesson 16

- ❏ Complete Chemical Processes Section Review
- ❏ Perform SWOT Analysis on CP Section Review
- ❏ Complete Full-Length 2
- ❏ Review Full-Length 2

In Lesson 16

- > Performance Evaluation
- > High-Yield Quantitative Reasoning
- > Practice Cooldown

To Do After Lesson 16

- ❏ Read Biological Processes Ch. 15–17
- ❏ Complete BP Ch. 15–17 End of Chapter Questions

Performance Evaluation

> You will likely find that there is more than you know than you don't know on the Quantitative Reasoning Section.
> The goal of this lesson is to identify areas where you have potential to *gain* points and develop strategies to strengthen those areas.

Evaluate how comfortable you are with each Quantitative Reasoning subarea by marking a 1 (low difficulty), 2 (medium difficulty), or 3 (high difficulty) next to each topic.

PROBLEM TYPE	TOPIC	DIFFICULTY
Basic Math	Basic Operations	
	Word Problems	
	Fractions, Percents, Decimals	
	Scientific Notation	
	Unit Conversion	
	Logarithms	
Algebra	Polynomial Equations	
	Exponents	
	Graphing	
	Absolute Value	
	Inequalities	
	Linear Equations	
	Probability	
	Statistics	
Precalculus	Functions	
	Function Composition	
	Inverse Functions	
	Maxima and Minima	
	Exponential Functions	
	Logarithmic Functions	
	Circular Equations	
	Complex Numbers	
	Vectors and Scalars	

LESSON 16: QUANTITATIVE REASONING 4

Calculus	Limits	
	Continuity	
	Derivative Rules	
	Transcendental Derivatives	
	Concavity	
	Related Rates	
	Implicit Differentiation	
	Integration Rules	
	Definite Integrals	

For each topic you have identified as high difficulty, determine why this area is difficult.

Difficult Topic 1: _____

Circle all of the following that apply. This topic is difficult for me because:
   a. I have not studied this material at all, to completion, or in a long time.
   b. I have studied this topic but don't understand it.
   c. I cannot remember the equations to use.
   d. I know the equations but don't understand how to use them.
   e. I don't understand the question being asked.
   f. I get confused about doing _____ when solving these problems.
   g. I always forget to _____ when solving these problems.

Difficult Topic 2: _____

Circle all of the following that apply. This topic is difficult for me because:
   a. I have not studied this material at all, to completion, or in a long time.
   b. I have studied this topic but don't understand it.
   c. I cannot remember the equations to use.
   d. I know the equations but don't understand how to use them.
   e. I don't understand the question being asked.
   f. I get confused about doing _____ when solving these problems.
   g. I always forget to _____ when solving these problems.

Difficult Topic 3: _____

Circle all of the following that apply. This topic is difficult for me because:
   a. I have not studied this material at all, to completion, or in a long time.
   b. I have studied this topic but don't understand it.
   c. I cannot remember the equations to use.
   d. I know the equations but don't understand how to use them.
   e. I don't understand the question being asked.
   f. I get confused about doing _____ when solving these problems.
   g. I always forget to _____ when solving these problems.

Difficult Topic 4: _____

Circle all of the following that apply. This topic is difficult for me because:
- a. I have not studied this material at all, to completion, or in a long time.
- b. I have studied this topic but don't understand it.
- c. I cannot remember the equations to use.
- d. I know the equations but don't understand how to use them.
- e. I don't understand the question being asked.
- f. I get confused about doing _____ when solving these problems.
- g. I always forget to _____ when solving these problems.

Difficult Topic 5: _____

Circle all of the following that apply. This topic is difficult for me because:
- a. I have not studied this material at all, to completion, or in a long time.
- b. I have studied this topic but don't understand it.
- c. I cannot remember the equations to use.
- d. I know the equations but don't understand how to use them.
- e. I don't understand the question being asked.
- f. I get confused about doing _____ when solving these problems.
- g. I always forget to _____ when solving these problems.

Difficult Topic 6: _____

Circle all of the following that apply. This topic is difficult for me because:
- a. I have not studied this material at all, to completion, or in a long time.
- b. I have studied this topic but don't understand it.
- c. I cannot remember the equations to use.
- d. I know the equations but don't understand how to use them.
- e. I don't understand the question being asked.
- f. I get confused about doing _____ when solving these problems.
- g. I always forget to _____ when solving these problems.

Difficult Topic 7: _____

Circle all of the following that apply. This topic is difficult for me because:
- a. I have not studied this material at all, to completion, or in a long time.
- b. I have studied this topic but don't understand it.
- c. I cannot remember the equations to use.
- d. I know the equations but don't understand how to use them.
- e. I don't understand the question being asked.
- f. I get confused about doing _____ when solving these problems.
- g. I always forget to _____ when solving these problems.

LESSON 16: QUANTITATIVE REASONING 4

Now, let's develop a strategic plan to master each of these content areas.

(a)

(b)

(c)

(d)

(e)

(f)

(g)

High-Yield Quantitative Reasoning

> Recall the three stages of mastering Quantitative Reasoning problems:

1. Learn
2. Repeat
3. Optimize

> This lesson is an opportunity to master the most high-yield and most challenging math problems using guided practice to boost your Quantitative Reasoning score. Hold on tight!

Solve the following high-yield Quantitative Reasoning problems.

Scientific Notation

1. Evaluate $\dfrac{0.0000639 - 0.1100006}{8.96 \times 10^{-7}}$.

2. Which of the following is the closest value to $\sqrt{4 \times 10^{-5.6}}$: 0.0000114, 0.000209, 0.00317, or 0.0261?

3. Evaluate $\dfrac{(5.12 \times 10^{-4})^3}{(2.67 \times 10^{7})^2}$.

Unit Conversions

1. In a fictional currency, there are 16 niles in a prelda, 3 preldas in a zippy, and 5 zippies in a marco. A raincoat that costs 2 marcos and 10 zippies can also be purchased with how many niles?

2. California has 840 miles of coastline. If it costs $0.03 per meter of coastline each month to maintain the beaches, how much does the state government spend in a year on beach preservation? (1 mile = 1609 meters)

3. A beaker with a 5-inch diameter is being filled with water at a rate that raises the water level 1 inch per minute. If this continued indefinitely, what volume of water would be added to an infinitely tall beaker after 1 hour?

Word Problems

1. Half of the plants in Diana's garden are flowers, and the other half are vegetable plants. An early frost destroys 6 flower plants and ¼ of the vegetable plants, and rabbits eat 4 of the remaining vegetable plants until only 25% of the original number of plants remains. How many plants did Diana start with in her garden?

2. A motorist is trying to catch up to a cyclist headed in the same direction. The motorist is traveling at a speed of 48 miles per hour, and the cyclist is traveling at a speed of 12 miles per hour. If the cyclist is 144 miles ahead of the motorist, how long will it take for the motorist to catch up the cyclist?

3. Kenneth drives 6 miles north, then 8 miles directly east to pick up his colleague for work. They then drive 12 miles northwest at a 30° angle to the west direction and then 2 miles south. How far is Kenneth's work place from home if he were to drive straight home? (sin 30° = 0.5)

Logarithms

1. Evaluate $\dfrac{(\log(\frac{X}{Y})^4)(\log 10^x)}{\log x}$.

2. The pH scale is a logarithmic scale where pH= $-\log[H^+]$. If there is no limit to the concentration of $[H^+]$, what is the lowest possible theoretical pH?

3. Draw the graph of ln(x) below.

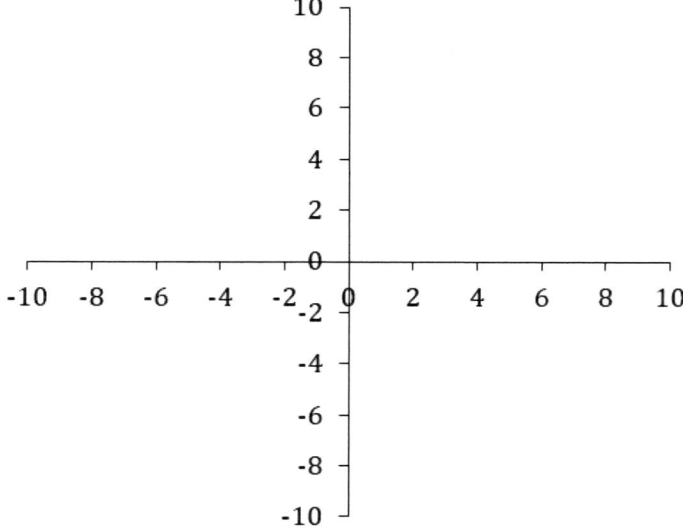

Probability

1. An individual with Disease X has a 50% chance of passing it on to each of her children. If she has 8 children, and each of her children has 6 children, what is the probability that all of her grandchildren will have Disease X?

2. Paul buys his lunch from a deli that offers 5 bread options, 3 kinds of meat, and 4 types of cheese. If he randomly chooses the ingredients to make his sandwich, what is the likelihood that Paul will order a turkey and provolone sandwich on either wheat or rye bread?

3. Lauren asks for volunteers from her class for a demonstration. If 8 girls and 7 boys raise their hands to volunteer and the volunteers are selected randomly, what is the probability that the second student she selects with be a girl?

Limits and Continuity

1. Find $\lim_{x \to 2} \frac{1}{x+2}$ and justify your response with a graph.

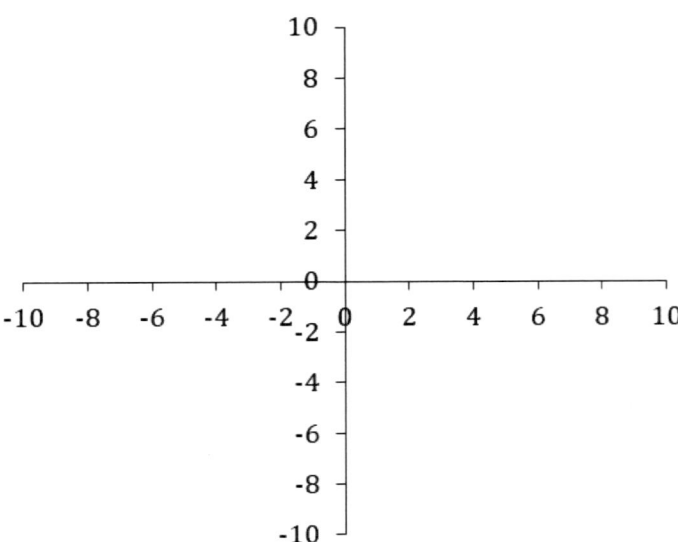

2. Find $\lim_{x \to 3} \frac{x^2-16}{x+4}$ and justify your response with a graph.

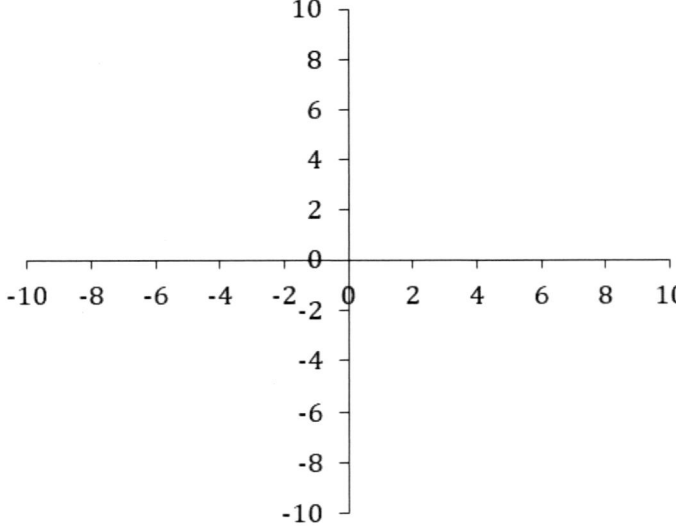

3. Find all discontinuities of the function $f(x) = \frac{x+1}{2x^3 - 8x^2 + 2x + 12}$.

Derivatives

1. Find the derivative of $\frac{6}{x^2}(1 - 3x)$ using the Product Rule.

2. Find the derivative of $(2x^2 - 1)^3$ using the Chain Rule.

3. Find the derivative of $(\cos x)(3x^2 + 2x + 1)$ at $x = 1$. ($\cos 1 = 0.540$ and $\sin 1 = 0.841$)

4. Find the maximum or minimum value of the function $f(x) = -9x^2 - 3x + 2$.

5. Find $\frac{dy}{dx}\left(y = \frac{4x^3}{y^2} - 3y^2\right)$.

Integrals

1. Find $\int \frac{3x(4x^3+x)}{2} dx$.

2. Find $\int_{-3}^{3} 9x^2 + 8x - 5\, dx$.

Practice Cooldown

1. Find $\frac{d}{dx}(3x \ln x)$.
   A. $3 \ln x$
   B. $\frac{3}{x}$
   C. $3 + 3 \ln x$
   D. $\frac{3 \ln x}{x}$

2. If there are three times as many red marbles as there are blue marbles in a bag, find the probability that a red marble will be randomly selected three times in a row, if it is replaced each time. Assume that the bag contains only red and blue marbles.
   A. $\frac{2}{3}$
   B. $\frac{3}{4}$
   C. $\frac{8}{27}$
   D. $\frac{27}{64}$

3. Find $\int (\sin x - 4x)\, dx$.
   A. $-\cos x - 2x^2 + C$
   B. $\cos x - 2x^2 + C$
   C. $-\cos x - 4 + C$
   D. $\cos x - 4 + C$

4. Find the inverse function of $f(x) = \frac{19 - x^2}{2x^2}$.
   A. $y = \sqrt{\frac{19}{2x+1}}$
   B. $y = \frac{x}{19 - x^2}$
   C. $y = \sqrt{\frac{2x+1}{19}}$
   D. $y = \frac{2x+1}{19}$

5. Find $\frac{d}{dx}\left(\frac{x}{4} - 9\right)^3$.
   A. $3\left(\frac{x}{4} - 9\right)^2$
   B. $\frac{1}{64}$
   C. $\frac{3}{4}\left(\frac{x}{4} - 9\right)^2$
   D. $\frac{1}{4}\left(\frac{x}{4} - 9\right)^4$

To Do After Lesson 16

❏ Read Biological Processes Ch. 15–17
❏ Complete BP Ch. 15–17 End of Chapter Questions

The Road to Test Day

LESSON 17

To Do Before Lesson 17

- ❏ Read Biological Processes Ch. 15–17
- ❏ Complete BP Ch. 15–17 End of Chapter Questions

In Lesson 17

- > Full-Length Review
- > Road to Test Day: Now
- > Road to Test Day: One Month Away
- > Road to Test Day: One Week Away
- > Road to Test Day: One Day Away
- > Road to Test Day: Game Day
- > Road to Test Day: Day After

To Do After Lesson 17

- ❏ Perform a global SWOT Analysis
- ❏ Re-evaluate your PCAT goals
- ❏ Develop a Road to Test Day Schedule
- ❏ Schedule your remaining Full-Length Exams
- ❏ Read Biological Processes Ch. 18–19
- ❏ Complete BP Ch. 18–19 End of Chapter Questions
- ❏ Complete the Biological Processes Section Review
- ❏ Study your LLJ

Full-Length Review

> Full-Length Exams allow you to practice both passage-based and discrete questions covering a broad range of content areas
> Full-Length Exams also give you an opportunity to build stamina and troubleshoot your pacing under timed conditions
> Reviewing and analyzing Full-Length Exams will help you improve your performance by developing strategic action items

Scheduling

Answer the following questions about scheduling Full-Length Exams.

How many Full-Length Exams should I take before Test Day? _____

How many weeks are left before Test Day? _____

How often should I schedule Full-Length Exams? _____

In what order should I take the Full-Length Exams? _____

Analyzing Your Score Report

Ask yourself the following questions about each question you missed on your most recent Full-Length Exam.

- ❏ What content knowledge, if applicable, could I have used to answer the question correctly? Why didn't I know this content information?
- ❏ What strategies, if applicable, could I have used to answer this question correctly? Why didn't I use these strategies?
- ❏ What shortcuts could I have used to answer this question more efficiently? Why didn't I use these strategies?
- ❏ Could I have answered this question correctly? What would I need to do differently?
- ❏ Does this fit a pattern or trend for reasons I have answered questions incorrectly on other exams?
- ❏ What things did I do *well* on questions I did answer correctly?

Use your most recent Full-Length Exam to analyze your score report.

SECTION	CURRENT SCALED SCORE (%ILE)	GOAL SCALED SCORE (%ILE)	# %ILE POINTS TO IMPROVE PER MONTH UNTIL TEST DAY
Composite			
Biological Processes			
Chemical Processes			
Critical Reading			
Quantitative Reasoning			

BIOLOGICAL PROCESSES	# Q'S MISSED DUE TO . . .	BIG PICTURE	ACTION STEPS
Content Errors		> > > > >	1. 2. 3. 4. 5.
Critical Reasoning Errors		> > > > >	1. 2. 3. 4. 5.
Careless Errors		> > > > >	1. 2. 3. 4. 5.
Timing Issues		> > > > >	1. 2. 3. 4. 5.
Other		> > > > >	1. 2. 3. 4. 5.

LESSON 17: THE ROAD TO TEST DAY

CHEMICAL PROCESSES	# Q'S MISSED DUE TO . . .	BIG PICTURE	ACTION STEPS
Content Errors		> > > > >	1. 2. 3. 4. 5.
Critical Reasoning Errors		> > > > >	1. 2. 3. 4. 5.
Careless Errors		> > > > >	1. 2. 3. 4. 5.
Timing Issues		> > > > >	1. 2. 3. 4. 5.
Other		> > > > >	1. 2. 3. 4. 5.

CRITICAL READING	# Q'S MISSED DUE TO . . .	BIG PICTURE	ACTION STEPS
Content Errors		> > > > >	1. 2. 3. 4. 5.
Critical Reasoning Errors		> > > > >	1. 2. 3. 4. 5.
Careless Errors		> > > > >	1. 2. 3. 4. 5.
Timing Issues		> > > > >	1. 2. 3. 4. 5.
Other		> > > > >	1. 2. 3. 4. 5.

LESSON 17: THE ROAD TO TEST DAY

QUANTITATIVE REASONING	# Q'S MISSED DUE TO . . .	BIG PICTURE	ACTION STEPS
Content Errors		> > > > >	1. 2. 3. 4. 5.
Critical Reasoning Errors		> > > > >	1. 2. 3. 4. 5.
Careless Errors		> > > > >	1. 2. 3. 4. 5.
Timing Issues		> > > > >	1. 2. 3. 4. 5.
Other		> > > > >	1. 2. 3. 4. 5.

NextStepTESTPREP.com

Using Your Lessons Learned Journal

Identify three discrete action steps you can take in the next month to answer 5–10 more questions correctly in each section.

Biological Processes
1.
2.
3.

Chemical Processes
1.
2.
3.

Critical Reading
1.
2.
3.

Quantitative Reasoning
1.
2.
3.

LESSON 17: THE ROAD TO TEST DAY

Pacing, Endurance, and Timing

Answer the following questions about timing on Full-Length Exams.

How much time would you need added to each section to finish with 5 minutes remaining before reviewing your answers?

Biological Processes _____

Chemical Processes _____

Critical Reading _____

Quantitative Reasoning _____

For each section, where do you miss the most questions (beginning, middle, end, or evenly distributed)?

Biological Processes _____

Chemical Processes _____

Critical Reading _____

Quantitative Reasoning _____

If you said . . .

> **beginning**, you might be rushing at the beginning of this section or need to be warmed up first. Try answering a few EASY questions before the test to warm yourself up, or doing light exercise or meditation beforehand to calm any nerves. Force yourself to be more diligent with checking your answers and reading—not skimming—passages at the beginning of the exam. Pace yourself for the long run!

> **middle**, you might be losing focus during the middle of the exam without the adrenaline spike at the beginning and end of each section. Work on active reading strategies, develop a plan for how often you will check the clock, and make sure that you take advantage of each full break. Imagine yourself as a sleuth investigating each question, or as a pharmacist analyzing data to help you prescribe the right medications. Too much adrenaline can cause you to rush, but too little will make the test boring!

> **end,** you might feel rushed towards the end of the exam. This is the most common pacing issue PCAT students encounter. Your first goal should be to try to identify any places where you can save on time (passages, questions, math shortcuts, etc.) or if you are spending too long on certain questions. Some students find it helpful to start off at a brisk pace and check the clock regularly so that you can adjust your pacing as you go. If little time remains, make sure that you have practiced Panic Mode strategies so you can do your best on the remaining questions. No question should go unanswered because there are no penalties for wrong answers on the PCAT! It is also possible that loss of endurance could be at play here—taking multiple Full-Length exams can help you build stamina and ward off fatigue on Test Day.

> **evenly distributed,** then you are very likely right where you want to be! Of course, you can always work towards giving yourself more of a time buffer to review your answers and prepare yourself for particularly tricky or long passages, but going too fast can also put you at risk for making mistakes.

Complete the table below with strategies you can employ can improve your pacing, endurance, and timing on Test Day.

PACING	ENDURANCE	TIMING

Road to Test Day: Now

> Whether Test Day is in one year or one week, it's never a bad time to plan ahead

Calibrating Your Study Plan

1. Count the number of weeks until Test Day and number each week in your calendar.

2. Make sure that the day before Test Day and at least one day per week are reserved as rest days, and add any extra rest days you might need to avoid burnout.

3. Determine how many additional Full-Length exams you will take and space them out equally until Test Day, with at least 4 days between each Full-Length. Plan to analyze each Full-Length that day or the following.

4. Create a checklist of priority content topics you wish to review before Test Day and a checklist of strategy goals before Test Day. Focus on at least one *specific* strategy goal with each practice passage.

5. Assign a subject area or content topic(s) to review each day from your priority content areas. Rotate content areas so that you do not study for the same section several days in a row. At the end of each review session, re-evaluate your priority content topics and add any new ones.

6. Develop a daily checklist for each day, which may or may not include:
    a. Content review
    b. Practice questions } *Rinse and repeat*
    c. Review practice questions
    d. Read X passages
    e. Review flashcards
    f. Write a 30-min essay from a practice prompt
    g. Review Lessons Learned Journal

Utilizing Your Resources

Identify your go-to resources for each of the following.

Content Review

NextStepTESTPREP.com

Practice Questions

Practice Passages

Practice Exams

Road to Test Day: One Month Away

Test-Friendly Habits

Create a realistic schedule for yourself by marking the analog clocks below with the following activities: wake time, sleep time, breakfast, lunch, snack, dinner, study period(s), break(s), and free time.

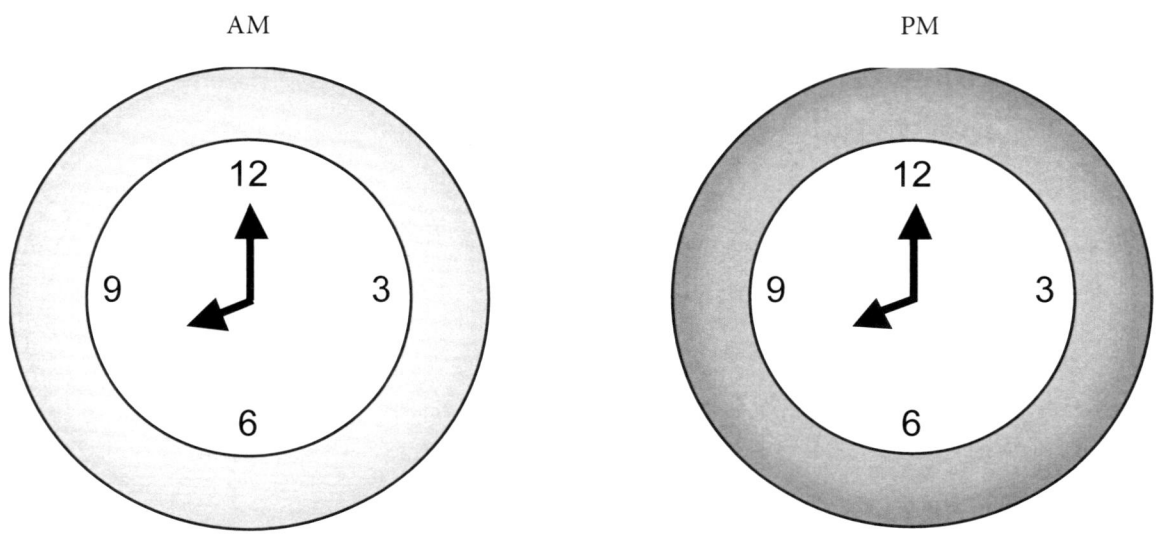

List food items and drinks that will keep you energized and hydrated while studying and on Test Day.

Commit yourself to preventing and recovering from burnout.

I will take a break from studying for _____ if I notice any of the following signs of burnout:

> **Example:** *drop in test scores, fatigue, change in mood, feeling stressed, etc.*

> _____

> _____

> _____

To prevent burnout, I will: _____.

To recover from burnout, I will: _____

How comfortable do you feel using each of the computer-based tools (1 = not comfortable at all, 5 = very comfortable)?

Typing an essay	1	2	3	4	5
Dry-erase board and marker	1	2	3	4	5
Standard online calculator	1	2	3	4	5
Periodic table	1	2	3	4	5
Countdown timer	1	2	3	4	5
Flag for Review button	1	2	3	4	5
Review Screen	1	2	3	4	5

Road to Test Day: One Week Away

10 Questions Until Test Day

1. Have you been implementing healthy habits to prepare for Test Day?
   _____
   _____

2. What resources, if any, have you under-utilized?
   _____
   _____

3. What content areas do you have concerns about in each section?
   _____
   _____

4. What other concerns (strategy, timing, endurance) do you have in each section?
   _____
   _____

5. What goals would you like to accomplish over the next week?
   _____
   _____

LESSON 17: THE ROAD TO TEST DAY

6. What confidence-building activities would you like to use over the next week?
   _____
   _____

7. Do you know the order and timing of the PCAT sections? Are you comfortable using the computer-based tools?
   _____
   _____

8. Do you know how to get to the testing center? Do you know what you will bring to the testing center?
   _____
   _____

9. What are your target and ideal PCAT score on Test Day? _____

10. What are you going to do the day before Test Day? _____
    a. No really, what are you going to do before Test Day?
    _____

Road to Test Day: One Day Away

> We *really* recommend that you take a Rest Day before Test Day
> Take Rest Day seriously! Active recovery will help you feel reenergized on Test Day. Here are some ideas:

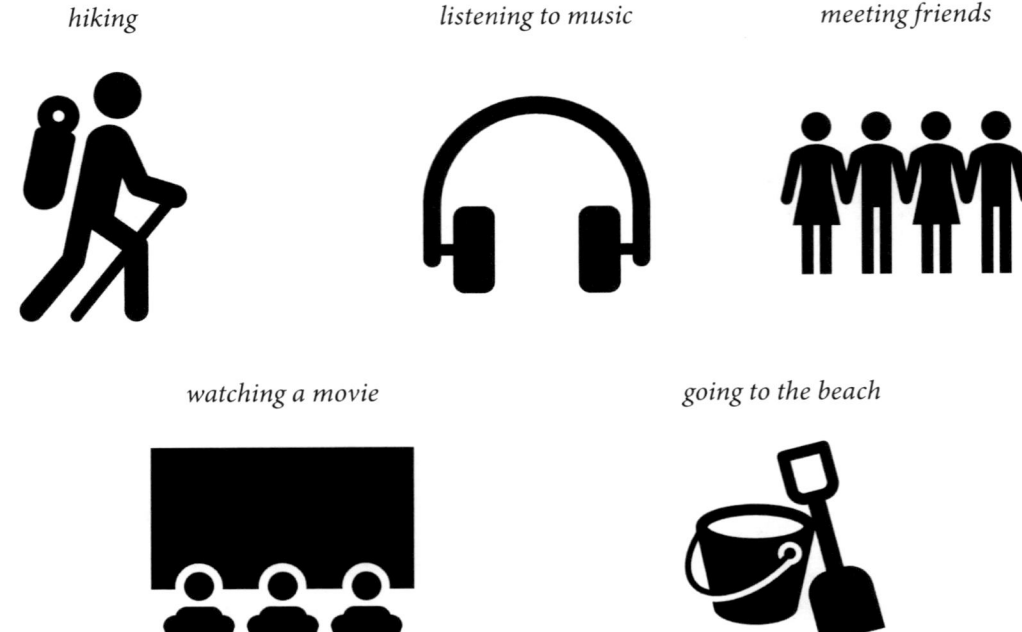

If you would feel *more* anxious not doing anything PCAT-related the day before your exam, you can:

> Answer a few, easy practice problems to boost your confidence
> Passively review your flashcards
> Skim your LLJ for high-yield strategies
> Pack the items you will bring to the testing center
> Practice driving to the testing center
> Schedule in rest and relaxation as *part* of your PCAT preparation

Road to Test Day: Game Day

What strategies can I use on Test Day to combat test anxiety?

What items will I bring to the testing center?

How will I get ready before my exam (time to wake up, time to leave, etc.)?

When will I receive my test scores?

What will I do after my PCAT?

Road to Test Day: Day After

> Your hard work is over, so this is a great time to celebrate!
> This is also an important time to reflect and plan your next steps.

After receiving your score report, below what score threshold would you want to re-take the PCAT, and when? What other options would you consider if you score below your target score?

With the PCAT under your belt, what steps must you take to complete your application to pharmacy schools? What timeline do you envision for this?

Practice Cooldown

1. All of the following statements are true of viruses EXCEPT:
   A. they are composed of proteins and nucleic acids.
   B. they often mutate at a high rate.
   C. they contain a number of simple membranous organelles.
   D. they are incapable of replicating without a host cell.

2. Down syndrome is a genetic condition that appears in about 0.1% of infants born each year. Also known as trisomy 21, it is caused by a genetic error in early development. What phenomenon and resulting genotype may be responsible for Down syndrome?
   A. Chromosomal crossover results in an embryo with two copies of chromosome 21.
   B. Chromosomal crossover results in an embryo with three copies of chromosome 21.
   C. Nondisjunction results in an embryo with three copies of chromosome 21.
   D. Nondisjunction results in an embryo with one copy of chromosome 21.

3. The level of cyclin and Cdks rise and fall during the cell cycle. What would be the consequence to a cell that, due to a missense mutation, displays perpetually high levels of both cyclin and Cdks?
   A. The cell cycle would cease entirely.
   B. The cell would be unable to divide.
   C. The cell would be arrested in the G_0 phase.
   D. The cell would rapidly move through the phases of the cell cycle.

4. Which of the following symptoms would be expected in someone with increased parathyroid gland activity?
   A. Decreased bone density
   B. Decreased blood calcium levels
   C. Increased metabolic rate
   D. Decreased metabolic rate

5. Is a halogen more likely to be reduced or oxidized, and why?
   A. Reduced, because a halogen will gain one electron to fill its valence shell.
   B. Reduced, because a halogen will lose one electron to fill its valence shell.
   C. Oxidized, because a halogen will gain one electron to fill its valence shell.
   D. Oxidized, because a halogen will lose one electron to fill its valence shell.

6. An unknown organic compound weighing 1980 mg is fully combusted at high pressure, yielding 900 mg of carbon dioxide and 360 mg of water. What is its empirical formula?
   A. $C_2H_4O_{10}$
   B. CH_2O_5
   C. CHO_3
   D. CH_6O_{10}

7. To enhance the flavor of a homemade soda, 49 g of phosphoric acid (H_3PO_4) is mixed with 2 L of carbonated water. If the density of the water is 1.5 g/mL, what is the solution's molality?
   A. 0.02 m
   B. 0.17 m
   C. 0.25 m
   D. 2.00 m

8. Find the inverse function of $f(x) = 3x^3 + 10$.
   A. $f(x) = \sqrt[3]{\frac{x-10}{3}}$
   B. $f(x) = \frac{1}{3x^3+10}$
   C. $f(x) = 3y^3 + 10$
   D. $f(x) = \sqrt[3]{3x - 10}$

9. Find $f''(x)$ given the function $f(x) = 4x^3 + \frac{x^2}{2} - 4x - 5$.
   A. $f''(x) = 24x + 1 + C$
   B. $f''(x) = 12x^2 + x - 4$
   C. $f''(x) = x^4 + \frac{x^3}{6} - 2x^2 - 5x + C$
   D. $f''(x) = 24x + 1$

10. What is the range of the function $f(x) = \frac{x^2-4}{x+2}$?
    A. All real numbers except $x = -4$
    B. All real numbers except $y = -4$
    C. All real numbers except $x = -2$
    D. All real numbers except $y = -2$

To Do After Lesson 17

- ❏ Perform a global SWOT Analysis
- ❏ Re-evaluate your PCAT goals
- ❏ Develop a Road to Test Day Schedule
- ❏ Schedule your remaining Full-Length Exams
- ❏ Read Biological Processes Ch. 18–19
- ❏ Complete BP Ch. 18–19 End of Chapter Questions
- ❏ Complete the Biological Processes Section Review
- ❏ Study your LLJ